Picks!

The Colorful Saga of Vintage Celluloid Guitar Plectrums

by Will Hoover

Miller Freeman Books

San Francisco

Published by Miller Freeman Books
600 Harrison Street,
San Francisco, CA 94107
Publishers of GPI Books, *Guitar Player, Bass Player* and
Keyboard magazines
A member of the United Newspapers Group

Distributed to the book trade in the U.S.
and Canada by
Publishers Group West,
P.O. Box 8843,
Emeryville, CA 94662

Distributed to the music trade in the U.S.
and Canada by
Hal Leonard Publishing,
P.O. Box 13819,
Milwaukee, WI 53213

Library of Congress Cataloging in Publication Data:
Hoover, Will.
    Picks! : the colorful saga of vintage celluloid guitar
plectrums / by Will Hoover.
        p.   cm.
    Includes bibliographical references (p.101) and index.
    ISBN 0-87930-377-8 (alk. paper)
    1. Plectra (Music) 2. Guitar--History.
ML1001.H66 1995
787.87' 19--dc20   [M]   95-18604

Printed in Singapore
95 96 97 98 99   5 4 3 2 1

TABLE OF CONTENTS

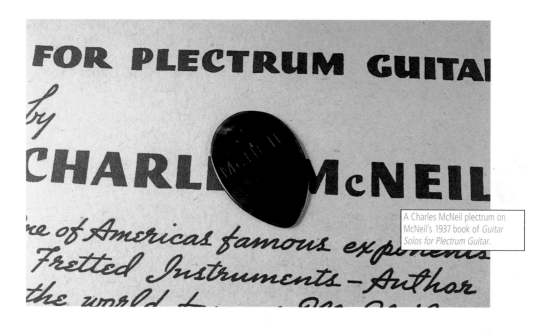

PREFACE

Picks. Funny little things. Nobody takes them seriously—confined to the musical periphery as picks are. Unnoticed. Humble. Overshadowed by performer and instrument. Residual servants that go about their task without fanfare, never to be included in a bow or curtain call. Ready to serve without notice, day or night. Asking nothing, loyal as Old Dog Tray.

Unnoticed. But not altogether unloved.

"People are married to their pick," said Collier Thelen, who operates a music shop on the Big Island of Hawaii. "They carry it in their wallet because it's their perfect pick, and they don't make 'em that shape anymore. And if they lose it, they grieve. Picks are an important part of the guitar, you

One of the largest celluloid plectrums ever made was the two-inch No. 366 mandolin and banjo pick.

Exclamation point made of two D'Andrea picks—Numbers 366 and 358 ¹/2.

Left, a post-Golden Age example of a celluloid mosaic or "assorted color" pick.

know. They're where the tone comes from. And yet, they are relegated to the edges of the shop and are not mentioned. Think of the great picks that are lying around forgotten in old guitar cases!"

One might imagine picks are an expendable item in the grand scheme of things. But then, imagine a world with no picks. Nothing but muted mandolins and bare-fingered banjos. No sounds of Doc Watson, Chet Atkins or Stevie Ray Vaughan. Imagine every guitar without a pick. You might as well imagine a song without a tune.

Imagine where that would leave rock 'n' roll —or country, or jazz.

But there ARE picks. Fantastic picks of assorted shape and design—made of ebony and ivory, stone and silver. Kaleidoscopic, translucent celluloid picks in stunning colors. Miniature works of art. Engineering marvels, complete with fantastic inventions to insure that they won't escape fleeting fingers and fling off into space. Picks from today and nostalgic picks from yesteryear, when fish were jumpin' and the cotton was high.

And, until now, picks that were too shy to come out in the spotlight to be recognized. Let's celebrate these tiny music makers. Throw open those old guitar cases and finally—at long last— applaud picks!

Trapezoid-shape pick in variegated colors from the Golden Age of Celluloid Plectrums.

In its most common form, the standard guitar pick is a No. 351 medium "Fender Pick"—the most ubiquitous pick of all.

INTRODUCTION

"Plectra, not plectrums!," admonishes Roger Evans in *How to Play the Guitar*. Actually, either is acceptable, not that the average person—who hitherto has never heard of a plectrum, singular OR plural—could much care. The average person does know what a guitar pick is.

Known variously as the American "standard," "No. 351," or "Fender Pick" for its shape and size, in its most common form this one-inch, triangular stringed instrument plectrum is .71 millimeters thick and is made of celluloid, the first commercial plastic. While picks have been made of other substances, more have been made of celluloid than any other material and probably more than all other materials combined.

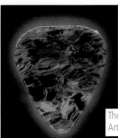

Right, in the summer of 1993 the Fender Guitar Company announced that it would begin phasing out its celluloid solid color picks, such as the one seen here.

The classic standard guitar pick. Art by Rob Dudley.

Celluloid is now made by only two major sources in the world, neither in the United States. Because of its beauty, strength, composition and "memory" (the ability to bend and return immediately to its original shape), celluloid has long been regarded by musicians as the superior material for picks.

Whether celluloid picks can endure, though, is in doubt. In the summer of 1993, the Fender Musical Instruments Co., whose name has long been synonymous with the standard celluloid guitar pick, issued a notice to its dealers that said in an effort to deal with the "crisis" of dramatically rising celluloid costs, the company would be phasing out its celluloid solid color picks and had been "working to find a substitute material that will provide the feel and durability of celluloid . . . ." Meanwhile, Jim Dunlop USA, one of the world's largest pick manufacturers, has quit making celluloid flat picks altogether. Pick Boy of Japan, another of the Big Three pick

makers, has drastically reduced its celluloid line. And D'Andrea, the world's largest celluloid pick manufacturer, is increasingly making picks of other plastics.

As one guitar dealer put it, "It will be the end of an era if they stop making picks of celluloid." But the Golden Age of Celluloid Plectrums has already come and gone. There are about a half dozen celluloid shapes currently on the market. By contrast, during the 1930s and '40s, D'Andrea offered varying color patterns in more than four dozen sizes and shapes—including picks with cork rings, corrugations and hand-"feathered" edges for professionals.

The search for the ultimate plectrum material is nothing new. Over the years picks have been made of ostrich, raven and eagle feathers, ivory, fibre, bone, coconut, stone, ebony, casein, brass and steel, not to mention tortoise shell and celluloid. In their quest to create a more perfect pick, inventors since the turn of the century have employed wire loops, holes, hold-

Nine non-celluloid guitar picks: top, left to right—bone, carbon fiber/plastic, cymbal brass, graphite/plastic and ceramic/plastic. Bottom—stone, ebony, rubber and coconut.

Over the years, numerous attempts have been made to create the perfect plectrum. This Kork-Grip pick, circa 1930s, was one of the more successful.

the story has never been told.

In the United States alone there are 19,000,000 guitar players. Most own at least one pick.

Left, Gorilla Snot adhesive pick rosin.

ers, twists, rubber plugs, sandpaper, notches, shanks, indentations, finger bands, multiple points, triple-decker fan shapes and a special flat pick adhesive rosin called "Gorilla Snot."

No one knows where old picks go to die. Some have merely retired to aging mandolin cases. Those that do make an appearance present a captivating tale. Equally fascinating,

While hundreds of common products have been made of celluloid since the turn of the 20th century, plectrums and table tennis balls are about the only ones that have never varied.

ACKNOWLEDGMENTS

This book was inspired by an event that had nothing to do with guitar picks. True, as an erstwhile troubadour, guitarist and recording artist, I'd owned my share of Fenders over the years. But what of them, really? A pick is just a pick. No, the impetus here was a vintage fountain pen fair in Honolulu, Hawaii in the early 1990s. It was at this affair that I encountered an assortment of writing instruments, with names like Waterman, Wahl Eversharp, Sheaffer and Parker, that had been produced between 1900 and the mid-1940s (1945 was the year a crafty entrepreneur named Milton Reynolds introduced something called a ballpoint pen—"Write on the ball!"—and overnight fountain pens became the stuff of romance).

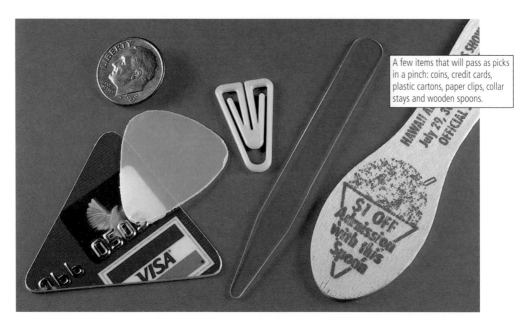

A few items that will pass as picks in a pinch: coins, credit cards, plastic cartons, paper clips, collar stays and wooden spoons.

What I saw at the fair were ink pens made of translucent plastics of striking design. Extraordinary plastics called Radite and Permanite and Pyralin. Plastics that at once left me mystified as well as vexed. "Why," I wondered, "can't plastics be made with such deep, rich colors anymore?" No one at the fair could offer an answer; I decided to find out.

Radite turned out to be the name Walter Sheaffer had anointed the material he used to produce the first commercial plastic pen in 1924. Further investigation revealed that the substance was identical to Permanite and

Pyralin—not to mention Fiberloid, Viscoloid, Herculoid and a host of other trade names individual manufacturing companies gave to the same material—celluloid. Most surprising was the fact that despite its strength, elegance and commercial appeal (no plastic has ever quite equaled it), celluloid exited the scene as an industrial material around the same time Reynolds' ballpoint rolled onto America's ink-stained arena. The reasons were many. Celluloid is excessively labor-intensive, requires months to cure and is so incendiary that no North American plastics

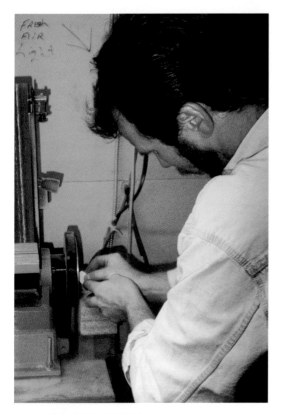

Midwest luthier John Hargiss making a mandolin plectrum from a scrap of "mother-of-pearl" celluloid.

manufacturer will even touch the stuff anymore.

Still, celluloid is not extinct. It continues to enjoy limited use in the manufacture of Ping-Pong balls. And guitar picks. What on Earth, I asked myself, could be the connection between these two common, though otherwise utterly unrelated, products? A cursory study of Ping-Pong balls bequeathed an expected array of findings: the ball was invented by James Gibb of England in the 1890s; Indian Industries of Evansville, Ind., the world's largest supplier of table tennis orbs, owns the name Ping-Pong; each U.S. Open Table Tennis Tournament paddles its way through 100 dozen balls—and so forth.

To my surprise, an attempted examination of guitar picks drew an unmitigated blank. Research librarians galore leafed through data bases at the speed of light and scratched their heads. Not so much as a treatise or thin volume on picks could be found. My curiosity tweaked, I launched a plectrum pursuit—an enterprise that carried me from Los Angeles to Saint Joe, Omaha to New York City, and back again. Piece by piece, a remarkable story, along with a lively cast of characters, emerged. Because there was scant written material about vintage celluloid picks, I frequently had to rely on the hazy recollections of those acquainted with the subject. Sadly, many principal players were no longer around, and those who were sometimes could offer no help. I spent weeks tracking down one old-timer who played a direct role in the pick saga, only to have him tell me he simply no longer remembered. I succeeded in locating the whereabouts of Luke Hart—undoubtedly an amazing character who devised several of the oddest plectrums ever made—only to be told he had died six months earlier.

The story presented here is as accurate as is possible under the circumstances. Often, I had to take whatever details were available and draw conclusions regarding those which were not. Nevertheless, assumptions were based on careful analysis.

Primarily, this book was a labor of affection. Having chanced upon a topic which had not been covered, I savored the opportunity to pursue it to a conclusion. The number of people who assisted me in this end is too long to list in total here. However, the following are those who made a special contribution and to whom I am most thankful:

First and foremost are Tony and Rosemary D'Andrea, without whom this book would not have been possible. They not only contributed vital background information about D'Andrea Manufacturing, but put me in contact with

others—including their competitors—who could add further insight. They provided many of the rare and vintage picks featured in these pages. Thanks also to Patrick McCaffery, Charlie Lusso, Marie Bartolozzi, Victor D'Andrea and the whole gang at the D'Andrea factory.

Special kudos go to two other individuals who supplied essential and hard-to-find pick catalog data dating back to the 1920s and before—Michael Lee Allen, a Chicago-area musician and music dealer, and Mike Mair of Vintage Paper in Platteville, Wisconsin.

I am especially indebted to Jerry Hershman for providing a detailed background of Herco, as well as a sense of the heady days of the music manufacturing industry from the 1940s through the 1970s. Similar thanks to Joe Moshay, Mel Bay, Jim Dunlop, Sam McRae, Tom Silva, Sidney Davis, Iler Ganz and Don Randall. My appreciation also to Julie Janac at

Celluloid plectrum handmade by John Hargiss.

Jaydee, Inc., Devin Duran of Skyline Unlimited, makers of LePik, and Greg Collins of Legend Picks.

The hundreds of vintage picks featured in this book came from scores of individual sources scattered across the country. In particular, I would like to say thanks to Omaha, Nebraska, luthier John Hargiss; Irvington, New York, vintage instrument dealer Sid Glickman; and Stanley Jay, president of Mandolin Bros. in Staten Island, New York. Collectors Harry Anderson Jr., of La Mirada, California; and Ilene Wong, Wayne Maeda, Kevin Dooley, Jim Danz, Neil Shimabukuro, Ernie Murphy, Emmett Yoshioka, Dennis Maeda and Mike O'Sullivan—all of Honolulu, Hawaii—contributed numerous rare picks.

For historical information on fretted stringed instruments, I am grateful to Mike Longworth, Richard Bruné, Walter Carter and George Gruhn. Pick inventors John Pearse, Bob Reineck, Steve Clayton and Larry Des Gaines were especially helpful. For providing understanding to the complexities of plastics, a tip of the fedora to writer R.J. Klimpert, as well as Nancy O'Keefe and Keith Lauer of the National Plastics Museum. Thanks to Paul Hettinger, Donnie Perkins, Tony Weathers, Jerry Coody, Mike Lowe and Jas Obrecht for escorting me through the world of celebrity imprint collectors.

And finally, for their considerable talents, advice, moral support and encouragement above and beyond the call, my humble appreciation to Cari White, Rob Dudley, Greg Yamamoto, John Strobel, Cheryl Dare, Ronn Ronck, Cory Lum, Theresa Oyama, Marsha Nakagawa, Mark Ryan, Bobby Bradford, Cathy Flanagan, Earl Shigemoto, Nancy Benedict and David Childs.

The mandolin pick on the left is genuine tortoise shell; the one on the right is made of ivory.

Chapter 1

ARROWHEADS AND EIGHT-STRING BANJOS

The origin of the stringed instrument plectrum, like the wheel, fire and other monumental achievements, has been lost to antiquity. Some theorists argue that the first stringed instrument must have been a bow and arrow. Caught up in the fervor of a successful slaughter, the original picker and his Upper Paleolithic pals were moved to strike up the band. If there's truth in any of this, it stands to reason that the first pick should have been an arrowhead. As long as there has been a stringed instrument, there has probably been a musician willing to influence its tone and volume with a hunk of wood, rock or bone. If nothing else, an arrowhead resembles a pick. This conjecture is meaningful since it indicates picks could be old indeed. Scientists in Katanda, Africa, have unearthed what looks to be an intricate harpoon point and weekend plectrum fashioned by human fingers some 70,000 years ago.

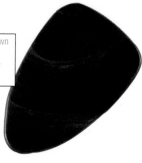

An oversize plectrum of unknown origin, possibly pre-1950s. It appears to be made of an early phenolic plastic, not celluloid.

We do know that plectrums (plectra to those who prefer plurals without an "s") have been around for ages. Stringed instruments that could have employed a plectrum appear in ancient Egyptian tomb carvings, and similar contrivances are known to have existed in locations from Africa to the Mediterranean to China 2,000 or more years ago. For centuries musicians have used a feather quill to pluck the oud, the lute of the Middle East and the classical instrument of the Arabian culture, which was introduced to the Spanish Peninsula with the invasion of the Moors in 711 A.D.

Feather quills, in fact, may have been the first standardized plectrums. They were pre-ferred pluckers among European troubadours of the Middle Ages, who strummed on musical devices similar to the mandolin. By the 1600s the French had become adroit at handling the Italian mandolla, which they plucked with a single finger to which a plume had been laced.

The Neapolitan mandolin itself has always required a plectrum. Ostrich feathers were favored in the late 1700s and early 1800s, although raven and corrette quills were acceptable. A solitary ostrich feather could produce up to five plectrums. An entire bird could bequeath a ten-year supply, plus dinner for 40.

According to those in the know, proper plectrums were expected to be elastic, never stiff, allowing the instrument to be played with "delicacy." To do so, the plectrum should be 40 to 60 millimeters in length and 1 millimeter thick. Flexibility could then be controlled and adjusted by holding the plectrum either nearer or farther from the tip. Those who were vexed by a quill's habit of fraying at the end could take comfort in the words of musician Leone de Naples: "It is wrong to trim the quill when it has become a little wispy," he wrote. "A little beard is always good, at least for making the notes more solemn and velvety."

Solemn, velvety notes notwithstanding, by the late 1800s quills had been upstaged by what many musicians came to regard as the superlative plectrum material—the outer casing of an Atlantic hawksbill sea turtle, otherwise known as tortoise shell. While everything from ivory to cherry bark had been tried, tortoise shell picks—made by hand from shells that had been heated and flattened - seemed to offer a most desirable combination of flexibility and tonal qualities when used to palpitate a taut strand.

Tortoise shell picks made in Europe were imported to America prior to the turn of the century. The first pick ever patented in the United States was a long, thin tortoise shell wedge "used to vibrate the strings of the banjolin," an 8-string banjo/mandolin combo designed in 1885 by John Farris of Hartford, Connecticut. It is of interest to note that Farris' pick was considered less of an accessory than a component of the banjo itself.

But other than their tendency to snap, tortoise shell picks had fundamental drawbacks. Foreign tariffs and hawksbill sea turtles being what they were, the stuff was expensive and supplies were limited. It was the sort of problem the manufacturing industry was facing with every manner of raw material, from ivory to rubber to silk. For those charged with supplying accessories to a growing population of minstrels, it necessitated the need to find an acceptable tortoise shell substitute. Plectrums were made from sole leather, ox horn and gutta percha, a hardened gum sap from the wild trees of Borneo. But these substances were lacking—too breakable, inflexible or not capable of achieving a desired tone.

The answer was to be found in an amazing new substance that was unlike anything the world had ever seen, a miracle man-made product that would spawn a colossal industry and radically alter society:

Celluloid—the first commercial plastic.

A celluloid billiard ball. It was the pursuit of a substitute for ivory billiard balls that prompted John Wesley Hyatt to invent celluloid in 1870.

Chapter 2

THE BALLAD OF JOHN WESLEY HYATT
AND FRANKENSTEIN'S PLASTIC

Dear Mr. Hoover:

I have heard you are writing a book on guitar picks. I wonder if you are aware that they can be deadly. During the 1980s, while living in Boston, I bought a 1957 Fender Stratocaster. One day, while practicing a subtle two-chord riff at top volume, I set my pick on a counter to see if a little finger picking would serve to embellish the lick. It did, and I became so excited I removed the lit cigarette from my mouth to better concentrate on my hands. I set it on the pick.

Moments later I heard a "whoosh!" and a thick cloud of whitish smoke began to rise from the pick. It was burning like the fuse on a stick of dynamite. I fled the room.

Please warn musicians to be careful not to hold a guitar pick near an open flame or lit cigarette. I shudder every time I see live concert footage of Jimi Hendrix lighting his guitar onstage. That man took incredible risks.

Yours truly,
Chris Neil

Chris is lucky he didn't burn down the whole Stratocaster. His reference to dynamite wasn't far off target. That pick he was using for a cigarette holder was made of a material that's a first cousin to guncotton, an explosive used in the American Civil War.

To understand why anyone would make a pick out of such volatile stuff, we must travel back to Albany, New York, in the late 1860s and meet printer John Wesley Hyatt, the son of a blacksmith, who was about to make a discovery. As one account goes, it happened while John was nursing a wound with a medicinal camphor ointment over which he had slathered collodion, a viscous solution that, once dried, formed a thin, waterproof bandage. Collodion had been used extensively on the battlefield earlier in the decade.

Meanwhile, over at Albany's firm of Phelan & Collender, officials were wrestling with a different dilemma: how to cope with a diminishing world ivory supply. Since the company was involved in the manufacture of ivory billiard balls, the issue was of no minor concern. Having failed to come up with a suitable alternative, Phelan & Collender tried another tack and offered a $10,000 prize for the patent rights to an ivory substitute. Hyatt, an enterprising young fellow, had endeavored to win what in those days amounted to a king's ransom by creating ivory-like materials of pressed wood pulp and gum shellac. While his pool balls weren't exactly impressive, his acquired proficiency in the ways of molding compounds under pressure was. Thus, while eyeing his injury, Hyatt was quick to spot what another person might have missed. His collodion bandage, which under normal circumstances tended to shrink and turn brittle, exhibited improved material characteristics with the addition of the ointment. Hyatt suspected the camphor had something to do with it.

Collodion was one of many products made from a compound called nitrocellulose—cotton fibers mixed with nitric acid—which has been around since 1846. Most notable among these products was the explosive guncotton, an insoluble substance. However, for years

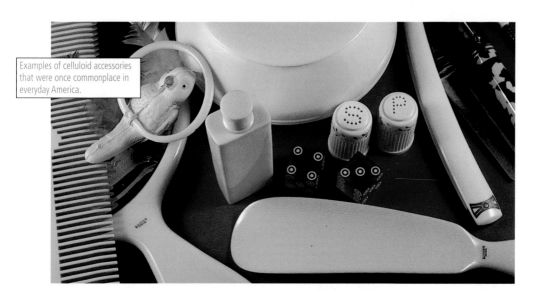

Examples of celluloid accessories that were once commonplace in everyday America.

scientists had known that in a less acidic form, nitrocellulose becomes a non-explosive, soluble goo—a highly flammable goo, to be sure—that can be converted into moldable solid materials. Trouble was, no one had ever found a plasticizer that would prevent the end result from shrinking and turning brittle. Inventors were motivated to continue their solvent search because the rewards seemed so promising. After all, cellulose (the cell walls of everything from grass to wood), is one of the cheapest, most abundant raw materials on earth. And in a world of decreasing natural materials, creating everyday products of plant cells would be good news indeed. So, every-

thing from linseed to castor oil was stirred through the nitrocellulose—always with less than stirring effects.

Hyatt made the necessary quantum leap in 1870 by not only mixing the correct solvent (camphor) with nitrocellulose, but doing so under heat and pressure. The result was celluloid—a product so revolutionary that for a time no one seemed to know what to do with it. Hyatt knew he was onto something, though, and had a ready source of supply with which to experiment: the government's Civil War gun-cotton stockpile.

Naturally, Hyatt attempted to produce celluloid billiard balls, but these didn't work well.

16

Before the advent of plastics, personal accessories were made from natural materials that were frequently rare and expensive, such as tortoise shell, ivory, exotic woods and precious metals.

According to at least one saloon owner out West, they had a habit of exploding when struck with sufficient force by another ball. It wasn't the blast that bothered the barkeep, Hyatt later recalled, "but that instantly every man in the room pulled a gun." So, with the assistance of his brother, Isaiah, Hyatt turned to making celluloid false teeth. These, too, were a losing enterprise since most people preferred to gum their food rather than chew it through the ever-present rancid-minty flavor of camphor.

In time, celluloid's magic ability to mimic natural substances was established and the plastics industry was born. At last, product manufacturers had an ample supply of quality working material. And what a material! Celluloid could not only look and feel like everything from mother-of-pearl to ebony, it could be fashioned into ultra-ordinary materials as well. Artisans, long since forgotten, cleverly exploited celluloid's unique translucency to create dazzling designs in rich, variegated colors. Since celluloid begins as a cool, dough-like substance, everything from dye swirls to gold flakes to microscopic fish scales could be incorporated into its patterns. Celluloid was never inexpensive in the sense that people think of plastics today. Tin and rubber, for example, were less costly. But celluloid was far more affordable than such exotic materials as ivory or tortoise shell, which were the domain of the affluent and privileged. Celluloid allowed the middle class to possess life's elegant, everyday articles. In so doing, it transformed the structure of society. The list of plastic prod-ucts was virtually endless and included cuffs,

There are literally thousands of different celluloid patterns. Here are three of many styles of celluloid "shell" designs.

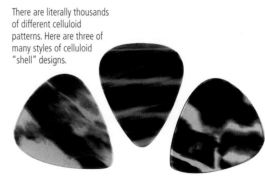

collars, razor handles, combs, thimbles, brushes, mirror casings, knobs, picture and eyeglass frames, dice, toys, novelties, compact cases, jewelry boxes, piano keys, photographic films, Ping-Pong balls and fountain pens.

In the case of stringed instrument plectrums, celluloid was singularly suitable. Where tortoise shell picks were scarce and expensive, celluloid picks could be had for a song. Nearly identical to tortoise shell in feel, appearance and timbre when laid to a string, celluloid improved on tortoise shell's flexibility. Celluloid picks could also be produced in any thickness gauge. More significant was celluloid's muscle power (it has the highest tensile strength of any thermoplastic material), and what is known in the plastics biz as "memory"—meaning its ability to be bent and return to its original shape instantly. Memory is essential in a plectrum because any pick suffering from amnesia will soon be out of sync in the split-second world of stringed instrument twang.

Celluloid mandolin picks were available by the turn of the century. Back porch pickers could order them for ten cents a dozen out of the 1907 Sears catalog—each pick guaranteed to be "very pliable and well adapted for tremolo." By that time, celluloid was already replacing tortoise shell as the primary pick material.

It is important to remember that while celluloid was the first commercial plastic, it was not the first synthetic material. Credit for that goes to Leo Hendrik Baekeland, who in 1909 transformed formaldehyde and carbolic acid into long chains of molecules called polymers. The first manmade compound formed completely by chemical reaction, Bakelite (which was as inappropriate for making plectrums as celluloid was for making billiard balls) paved the way for the synthetic materials revolution of the 20th century. Materials that, unlike celluloid, were relatively mild-mannered.

Celluloid, by contrast, is a semisynthetic material. Half natural, half unnatural. And in this light we discover its most fascinating and cryptic characteristic. Like Frankenstein's monster, Mary Shelley's infamous half natural, half unnatural creature, John Wesley Hyatt's creation possessed a dark side. Perhaps it is simply too much to expect the most beautiful plastic ever invented to be refined as well. Or, maybe it was simply The Call of the Guncotton. Whatever, celluloid remained forever erratic. For reasons no one seems able to explain, celluloid occasionally combusts spontaneously. It gnarls, warps, cracks, fades, liquefies, crystallizes, rots from the inside and otherwise goes hideous. It is hygroscopic, meaning it perpetually seeks moisture to which it is sensitive. It can be the model of stability for decades and then, without warning, turn bad. It can do all this on its own, without so much as a spark of outside interference. But introduce it to fire, its mortal enemy, and the outcome is always combustible. The list of factories handling celluloid that have gone up in flames during the 20th century is a long one.

For years celluloid makers waged a campaign to correct its diabolical disposition. Stabilizers were eventually added; the formula was modified. In the end, celluloid's major character defect—extreme volatility—could not be disciplined. Moreover, its fiendish mood shifts proved to be utterly unpredictable. Consequently, science focused on devising a plastic that would mimic the great copycat itself—the best being cellulose acetate, a nonflammable thermoplastic material that lacks celluloid's tensile strength and memory and is unsuitable for stringed instrument plectrums.

One by one, product manufacturers began turning to other plastics—acetate, acrylics and nylon. Where once there had been four giant celluloid manufacturers in America including DuPont, eventually there were none. Except for Italy and Japan, which continued to produce the first plastic, celluloid was for all practical purposes a thing of the past by the

While picks made of phenolic plastics such as bakelite were too stiff and brittle to be of great value, some bakelite picks—such as these three—have nevertheless been manufactured.

1940s (in the early 1990s, after a break of five decades, Italy and Japan began manufacturing celluloid fountain pens once more). Of the myriad products once made of celluloid, two holdouts remained: Ping-Pong balls and stringed instrument plectrums. The fate of the former seemed secure. As long as there was table tennis there would be celluloid Ping-Pong balls, for the simple reason that nothing else works (celluloid balls have been used exclusively since the game was first marketed in 1898). As for picks, the future is unclear. Two of the world's three largest pick manufacturers have moved away from celluloid; alternative materials, including composite plastics, are continually being tried. As yet, nothing has upstaged celluloid as the finest all-around pick material.

Then again, no other pick material goes "whoosh!" when you least expect it.

The Holy Grail of Guitar Picks: Luigi D'Andrea's original No. 351 mallet die from the 1920s. Notice that the distinctive one-inch, rounded-isosceles shape remained unchanged over the years. The Nick Lucas pick on the left is from the Golden Age of Plectrums. The D'Andrea pick on the right is from the 1990s.

Chapter 3

THE PICK WITH THE CROONING TONE

Shortly after 10 A.M. on January 23, 1994, at booth number 1614 at the National Association of Music Merchants Show in Anaheim, California, a one-pound chunk of hardened steel was reverently, though informally, removed from a tiny cardboard box. It was placed on a table top where it was photographed, possibly for the first time. The man holding the curious object was Tony D'Andrea, president of D'Andrea Manufacturing, the world's largest celluloid pick maker. The event went unheralded. All around, assorted ambassadors of the music industry—pockets bulging with free promotional guitar picks—paid slight attention to the item in question, marked only by a tiny strip of aging, yellow paper bearing the handwritten numerals "351."

Had passersby realized the significance of the object, they might have paused to pay homage. There, on the tabletop, lay The Holy Grail of Guitar Picks—an original D'Andrea mallet die from the 1920s—shape No. 351—from which the first guitar pick most likely sprang. Clearly discernible at the cutting end of the die was that distinctive one-inch rounded-isosceles triangle, recognized by guitarists the world over. The No. 351 shape itself had not varied in six decades. It remained the industry standard. That shape had been around since at least 1928, when Tony D'Andrea's grandfather, Luigi D'Andrea, offered it and some three dozen other pick shapes to music merchants.

Even as the die was being captured on film, standard guitar picks were being handed out freely at locations throughout the convention halls. Jim Dunlop, head of one of the Big Three pick-manufacturing companies, claims to have doled out 10,000 picks in a single hour that day. He may have exaggerated, but there's no question picks galore were being snapped up in a frenzy by the thousands in attendance.

Equally certain is the fact that few of the recipients were aware of the story behind the shape of guitar picks, nor that had it not been for "Tiptoe Thru the Tulips with Me," standard guitar picks might never have existed, and Elvis Presley, Les Paul and Eric Clapton might have ended up strumming on the ol' banjo.

Prior to the Roaring Twenties, guitars played a distant second fiddle to the mandolin in popularity. After World War I, the mandolin was rivaled by the tenor banjo. Six-stringed guitars remained a lesser-known commodity and were regarded as an instrument for backup rhythm accompaniment. Throughout the late 19th century and the first part of the 20th century in America, six-string guitars were principally gut-string classical-style instruments that were played with unadorned fingers. Although the Gibson and Martin companies were both manufacturing some steel string guitars by the 1920s, these were generally not played with a flat pick. Mississippi blues guitarists

Right, an early D'Andrea No. 360 mandolin and banjo plectrum.

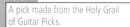

A pick made from the Holy Grail of Guitar Picks.

Gibson's Nick Lucas portrait from the 1930s.

Right, banjo thimbles ad from an early 1920s Wurlitzer catalog.

emporium were shown the thumb and finger-pick selection.

All that was about to change with the advent of radio, phonograph records, "the talkies," and a young vaudevillian named Nick Lucas. Born Nicolas Lucanese in Newark, New Jersey, on Aug. 22, 1897, Lucas was an accomplished musician by his teens, having mastered both the mandolin and banjo. But Lucas' legacy to the world of popular music would be his style of singing while playing the guitar with a flat pick.

Lucas started out in 1915 playing backup banjo and guitar with a band in Newark. In the early 1920s, for the Pathe label, he was the first person to record guitar solos on wax cylinders. One of those recordings was titled, "Pickin' the Guitar." Following successful tours in America and Europe in the early '20s, Lucas

such as Blind Lemon Jefferson and Robert Johnson employed a distinct finger-picking style, as did Southern country pickers Riley Pucket, Sam McGee and others. Flat picks or plectrums were strictly mandolin and banjo accessories. Musicians asking for "guitar picks" at their neighborhood music

entered the burgeoning medium of live radio via the Oriole Orchestra at Chicago's Edgewater Beach Hotel and became an overnight singing sensation. In 1925 he signed a contract with Brunswick Records, released several hits and, along with such artists as Gene Austin, Blossom Seeley and Johnny Marvin, pioneered a new form of intimate music that would make showcase legends of the likes of Rudy Vallee, Ruth Etting and Bing Crosby.

In 1929, Lucas landed a role in one of the first all-talkie Technicolor movies, Warner Brothers' *Gold Diggers of Broadway*. The musical featured tunes written by New York songwriters Al Dubin and Joe Burke, including "Tiptoe Thru the Tulips with Me," which Lucas warbled while playing the guitar with a flat pick as a chorus of young maidens frolicked through a field of artificial flowers. The audience loved it. Lucas, who by then was billed as "The Crooning Troubadour," had the smash of his life with "Tiptoe Thru the Tulips." Thanks to him, musicians were swapping their banjos and mandolins for six-string guitars, and the world of popular music would never be the same. Lucas, along with guitar virtuosos Eddie Lang and Roy Smeck, brought the steel-string guitar to the forefront as an instrument in its own right.

But Lucas made another contribution to

Nick Lucas and Winnie Lightner, from the 1929 film *Gold Diggers of Broadway*. Although no complete copies of the film exist, this still photo shows Lucas using what appears to be a plectrum to pick his guitar.

popular music that should not be underestimated. He established the guitar pick. Lucas used what came to be referred to as a "plectrum-style guitar pick." And although he may not have been the first guitarist to use a plectrum, he popularized the practice just as he popularized the six-string guitar itself. After Gibson's Nick Lucas Guitar was introduced, the Nick Lucas guitar pick made its debut. Sometime in the early 1930s, Joe Nicomede, friend and colleague of Luigi D'Andrea, worked out a

deal with Lucas. Nicomede, an Altoona, Pennsylvania, music teacher, agreed to pay Lucas a royalty to market flat picks bearing the Lucas name. D'Andrea agreed to manufacture the line. The shape Nicomede and Lucas chose was the No. 351, which in all probability D'Andrea designed himself, possibly with the help of Lucas. The finished product featured a stylized impression of the artist's name, the first guitar pick to bear an imprint. Unlike any pick before it, this unique design was exclusively associated with a guitarist. Thus, it became forever linked with the guitar. The No. 351 was, and still is, THE guitar pick. Like most D'Andrea shapes, the No. 351 shape was never patented—meaning anyone was free to use it. Nevertheless, for many years even competing pick marketers referred to it as the "Nick Lucas shape."

Known as "the pick with the crooning tone," Lucas picks retailed for 10 cents each, three for a quarter and came 24 picks to the display card. Hedging its bets, the card claimed to hold "Your choice of real banjo and guitar picks."

The picks were made of celluloid, although that fact was not mentioned on the card. Competition eventually came in many forms. Wabash and Milton O. Wolf guitar picks, for example, were the No. 351 shape. Guitarist Nick Manoloff's celluloid picks were not only the Nick Lucas shape, they were presented on a display card strikingly similar to the Lucas card. Even the celluloid No. 351-shape "Gene Autry plectrum-type guitar pick" offered in the 1941 Sears catalog wasn't able to threaten Lucas' claim to the guitar pick.

That honor goes to the Fender Company, which until the early 1950s had sold Nick Manoloff picks in its catalogs. However, Fender dropped Manoloff, so the story goes, when a top company representative arrived at an East Coast music trade show only to discover he had forgotten to bring guitar picks. The momentary crisis was alleviated when reps from the D'Andrea booth generously, and

While the Nick Lucas pick was the standard guitar pick for many years, after the mid-1950s more musicians knew it as Fender Medium guitar pick, also known as the "Fender Pick."

at no cost, supplied Fender with ample picks for the show. The incident supposedly led to the long relationship between Fender and D'Andrea and the beginning of the most ubiquitous guitar pick on earth, the Fender Medium, No. 351—known to guitarists everywhere as "the Fender pick."

Whether or not the story is true, it's a fact that in 1955 D'Andrea entered into an agreement to manufacture No. 351-shaped picks with the distinctive Fender logo, as well as Fender picks in various other shapes in thin, medium and heavy gauges. But it was the Fender Medium, No. 351, sometimes called the "sideman pick," that became universally recognizable.

A decade later the No. 351 shape was rarely equated with Nick Lucas, although his picks were still available. By then Lucas had faded from public view and was unknown to a new generation of musicians. One who remem-

This vintage "Famous No. 351" imprint was obviously made in honor of the guitar pick, which Luigi D'Andrea designed and Nick Lucas made famous—although it's unlikely that many guitarists understood the significance when D'Andrea Manufacturing made it in 1973 for Northeast, a distributor that has since gone out of business.

bered, though, was entertainer Tiny Tim, who claimed to have been inspired by the crooner. On December 17, 1969, Lucas sang his trademark song at Tim's wedding, which was broadcast nationally on the Johnny Carson "Tonight Show." At 40 million viewers, the program broke TV audience records.

Lucas died on July 28, 1982. And although his song has ended, the guitar pick lingers on.

Two celluloid boxes filled with early celluloid plectrums.

Chapter 4

PLECTRUM PIONEERS AND THE
FLYING PICK AFFAIR

Among those who use picks there has long been a perception that, given an opportunity, the common plectrum will escape the clutch of a musician's fingers and go airborne. It's said even picks that aren't frequent flyers have a nasty habit of shifting positions and otherwise turning on their masters. To insure that picker would maintain dominion over pick, a parade of dedicated plectrum pioneers entered the American scene around the turn of the century. Some, such as David W. Barnes of Brooklyn, New York, concentrated on tonal and shape improvements, and although his 1903 celluloid and

leather plectrum didn't catch on, it was a necessary link in the evolutionary plectrum chain. Others turned their attention to pick design. A year after Barnes' innovation was announced, Charles F.W. Seidel, also of Brooklyn, unveiled a multi-point plectrum that operated rather like a pocketknife. By using points individually or in conjunction with one another, musicians using Seidel's remarkable pick gained a variety of gauge and sound options. Barnes and Seidel were indicative of inventors who grappled with the functionality of a plectrum. More prevalent were those who concocted ways of preventing a pick from flipping out of a player's fingers.

Frederick Wahl of Cincinnati, Ohio, was such a person. In 1896 he analyzed the dilemma and devised what was probably the first serious attempt to control unruly fly-away plectrums. Wahl's apparatus, which retailed for around 15 cents, consisted of a pair of fingertip-size concave rubber discs between which a mandolin plectrum could be sandwiched. The discs were attached to a steel ring that was in turn affixed to a player's thumb. Cumbersome as Wahl's invention may have been, the idea was a hit. For years it was a regular offering of the Sears, Roebuck & Co. catalog, which praised its subtle attributes: "… By placing the thumb and index finger lightly on the disc the player will be able to

This unusual D'Andrea No. 84 plectrum, circa 1940s, combines a thin, medium and heavy pick and opens like a fan. The concept evolved from Charles F.W. Seidel's original 1904 multi-point pick.

A 1920s Wurlitzer catalog ad for the vacuum grip pick and Frederick Wahl's patented pick holder.

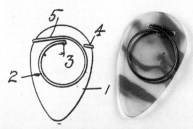

1,263,740. PICK FOR STRINGED INSTRUMENTS. AARON BURDWISE, Baltimore, Md. Filed Nov. 14, 1917. Serial No. 201,926. (Cl. 84—117.)

5. A pick for stringed instruments having an aperture therethrough, and a loop on each side of said pick in which the fingers rest, said loops being formed of wire passing through said aperture, the extremities being secured to said pick.

[Claims 1 to 4 not printed in the Gazette.]

Aaron Burdwise's 1917 patent application for his unique wire loop pick and the actual modified design. The Burdwise wire loop pick is also unusual in that it is one of the few picks that bears a patent date (too small to see here): April 23, 1918.

Two corrugated mandolin picks, circa 1940s. Right, close-up of a corrugated plectrum.

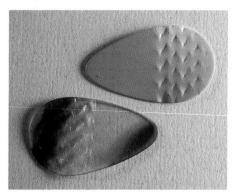
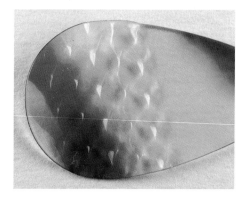

play the sweetest and softest music possible, and, if necessary, he can tremolo a chord with the utmost ease…" Eventually, the rights to Wahl's idea were bought by the Wurlitzer company, which continued the plectrum metamorphosis with its own invention, the Vacuum Pick, an improvement over Wahl's design that did away with the thumb ring by merely attaching a rubber suction cup to each side of a celluloid mandolin pick.

Slowly, plectrum architects were moving away from better pick-gripping devices to picks that could be better gripped. In 1900, Carolyn M. Cockrane of Buffalo, New York, fashioned a narrow shank through which a mandolin pick could be wedged. Although her idea was still a pick holder, it was far less complicated than Wahl's. Once a pick had been inserted into the shank, it became a pick with a belt that could be more readily clasped. A decade later, Louis Knackstedt of Annapolis, Maryland, devised an oblong celluloid plectrum with four rubber plugs protruding from both sides. Knackstedt's design was clearly a stand-alone plectrum with improved gripping capabilities.

Pick inventor Aaron Burdwise of Baltimore attacked the stabilization problem from a number of approaches. In 1917 he created a small celluloid pick with a wire loop on each side. This design was novel in that both loops were made from a single wire that was mechanically inserted through a hole in the pick and machine-twisted. Later, Burdwise patented an entire celluloid plectrum with a twist, "to fit the contour of the thumb and index finger when held therebetween," as well as a celluloid pick with felt attached to each side.

It was about this time that Richard Carpenter and Thomas Towner of Oakland, California, came to the conclusion that pick inventions themselves were getting out of hand. Why, they reasoned, must both sides of a pick be stabilized? If one side doesn't shift in a musician's fingers, neither will the other. Carpenter and Towner took a teardrop-shaped pick and glued a thin piece of nonslipping material to the rounded half of one side. The material they

All three Kork-Grip shapes, circa 1930s. The smaller picks were for mandolin, the larger shape for guitar or banjo.

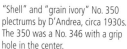

"Shell" and "grain ivory" No. 350 plectrums by D'Andrea, circa 1930s. The 350 was a No. 346 with a grip hole in the center.

chose was cork. Patented in 1915, the Kork Grip pick became popular with professional musicians who didn't mind paying twice the price for a pick they felt they could cling to. Cork, in fact, established itself as the favored pick-gripping material. For decades cork rings and pads were incorporated in numerous pick designs.

Luigi D'Andrea in the mid-1940s.

Not to be outdone, Peter Rudesyle of Passale, New Jersey, created a nonslip pick that had no added material whatsoever. His 1919 invention was nothing more than a one-piece flat pick with a wagon wheel of raised and lowered spoke surfaces at the rounded end of the oval, an effect that could be easily accomplished with celluloid. Rudesyle's concept was revolutionary. Realizing that pickers required nothing other than something to sink their fingerprints into, pick makers responded by creating celluloid wafers bearing everything from crosshatches to high-relief imprint logos.

And the person pickers have most to thank for providing such plectrums was the greatest pick pioneer of them all, Luigi D'Andrea—a Neapolitan bon vivant, amateur mandolin player and vacuum cleaner salesman. D'Andrea's contribution to the plectrum saga is so notable that picks could rightly be categorized either BD or AD (Before or After D'Andrea).

Heart-shape D'Andrea picks with cork grips, circa 1930s.

A pick made from Luigi D'Andrea's original heart-shape mallet die which he bought at a 1920 sidewalk sale. Note the similarity between this shape and the No. 351.

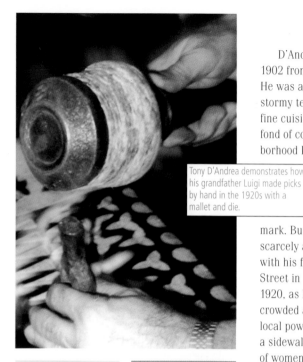

Tony D'Andrea demonstrates how his grandfather Luigi made picks by hand in the 1920s with a mallet and die.

D'Andrea immigrated to New York City in 1902 from Lamis, Foggia, Italy at age 17. He was a robust, passionate dreamer with a stormy temper and a zest for music, cigars and fine cuisine. At the height of his career he was fond of commandeering the kitchens of neighborhood Italian restaurants and personally preparing dinner for 30 or more friends and music business associates. Above all, D'Andrea was ambitious. He wanted to earn his mark. But following World War I, he earned scarcely a subsistence wage and was living with his family in a cold-water flat off Mott Street in New York's Little Italy. One day in 1920, as he beat his way through the dusty, crowded alleys, D'Andrea stumbled across a local powder puff manufacturer in the midst of a sidewalk distress sale. Intrigued by the stuff of women's compacts, he traded his pocket change for a sheet of "tortoise shell" celluloid, a mallet and several knife dies from which tiny compact decorations were cut. At that moment D'Andrea realized his destiny: to corner the women's powder puff market.

Fortunately for the world of fretted stringed instruments, things didn't work out that way. After the compact enterprise proved no more rewarding than hawking carpet cleaners, D'Andrea sat down at the kitchen table, drum-

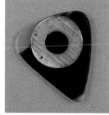

Left, a D'Andrea corrugated plectrum, circa 1950s.

Right, a D'Andrea No. 46 cork grip pick featured in the company's 1928 catalog.

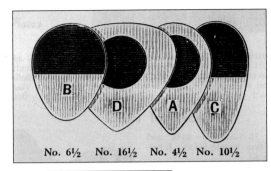

No. 6½   No. 16½   No. 4½   No. 10½

Above, A 1933 catalog ad for Gretsch "Non-Skid" picks.

Luigi D'Andrea experimented with numerous shapes. These two from the 1920s—an ice-cream-cone-shape and a pick with three different points—are not found in any known catalog listings.

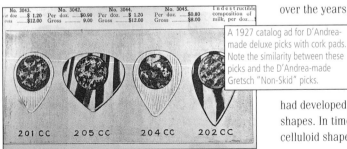

No. 3043.	No. 3042.	No. 3044.	No. 3045.	Indestructible composition of milk, per doz.....
r doz .....$ 1.20	Per doz. $0.90	Per doz. ...$ 1.20	Per doz. $0.80	
oss $12.00	Gross 9.00	Gross $12.00	Gross $8.00	

201 CC   205 CC   204 CC   202 CC

A 1927 catalog ad for D'Andrea-made deluxe picks with cork pads. Note the similarity between these picks and the D'Andrea-made Gretsch "Non-Skid" picks.

med his fingers and pondered his compact decorations. "They look like cousin Primo's mandolin picks, Papa," remarked Anthony, his 9-year-old son. Thus inspired, D'Andrea loaded up a box of one-inch heart-shaped chips and headed off to the Manhattan music publishing firm of G. Schirmer and Company. Because his English was poor, young Anthony was dragged along to translate. The result was a $10 sale and the humble beginnings of the world's largest pick company.

D'Andrea Manufacturing started out in 1922 in a one-room loft at 395 West Broadway, which, in the words of the founder, was "the size of the scene in the second act of *La Bohème*." There, D'Andrea pounded out celluloid plectrums while his son hand-beveled the edges with a belt sander. Luigi and Anthony were later joined by Anthony's brother Victor, and then by sister Eda. While Anthony furnished most of the company's business aplomb over the years, his father, a creative dynamo, provided the inspiration. Prior to 1922 there had been about a half dozen different oval-shaped plectrums on the market. By 1928 D'Andrea had developed more than three dozen different shapes. In time, that number increased to 56 celluloid shapes plus 23 styles of genuine tor-

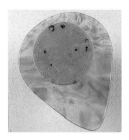

Left, a striking No. 349 cork grip pick from the Golden Age.

A D'Andrea heart-shape mosaic. Circa 1930s.

Below, an "unfinished" mandolin pick of unknown origin. Circa 1920s.

Above,, an example of a deluxe pick with a hand-beveled edge. The origin of this extremely thick plectrum is unknown. Circa 1930s.

toise shell picks (in addition to celluloid thumb and finger picks and felt ukulele picks). Suddenly, music dealers were offering oval, triangle, trapezoid, teardrop, curved, oblong, five-sided and triple-pointed picks that came either plain or "De Luxe," and with a choice of corrugations, cork rings, pads, center holes, plugs, rubber cushions and grommets. It mattered not to D'Andrea if picks could fly, but only that there was a plectrum to match every picker's whim and fancy. D'Andrea listened to musicians' pick suggestions and incorporated them with his own innovations to produce a product array unlike anything that preceded it.

Ironically, one pick D'Andrea didn't keep was the original heart shape. In its place, he created a slightly smaller pick that was virtually identical except that the heart was closed at the top and the opposing sides were straightened. This pick, which D'Andrea origi-

nally dubbed the No. 44, was later called the No. 351. It would become the most familiar pick shape of them all.

Throughout the 1930s, '40s and '50s, D'Andrea Manufacturing dominated the world's wholesale pick market, unchallenged by any major competitor. D'Andrea cornered the lucrative O.E.M. business (it stands for original equipment manufacturers, which, in this instance, meant such instrumental giants as Gibson, Martin, Fender and Gretsch, for whom D'Andrea made picks). The company

A distinctive trapezoid plectrum, circa 1920s.

Far left, large Golden Age "grain ivory" plectrum of unknown origin.

Left, a pair of Golden Age D'Andrea "grain ivory" No. 347 ¾ picks.

Right, deluxe Golden Age "grain ivory" No. 346 pick.

established the pick imprint industry, standardized pick thickness gauges and was the only outfit in America to make genuine tortoise shell picks (a practice the company ended in the mid-1970s when hawksbill turtles hit the endangered species list).

For much of this period, D'Andrea Manufacturing was content to supply picks for the industry while staying in the background. Few musicians realized that whatever brand of pick they were using, in all probability it had been made by D'Andrea. The seven-page Guitar, Mandolin and Banjo Picks section of the 1949 catalog from David Wexler & Co., a Chicago-

A pair of unique comma or "finger-shape" mandolin plectrums from the Golden Age.

based musical supply house, was typical. In addition to celluloid picks from Wexler's own Wabash and generic house brands, the catalog listed celluloid picks from Nick Lucas, Nick Manoloff, Bob Clifton, George Barnes and DA Products—all of which were made by D'Andrea. DA Products, of course, was D'Andrea's own brand, but nowhere on the display or picks was the D'Andrea name mentioned.

It wasn't until the mid-1960s that D'Andrea got its first taste of rivalry. It came about largely because of the inventions of the last of the great pick pioneers—Joseph Moshay of Beverly Hills, California. Moshay's most noted plectrum contribution seemed like nothing, really. In fact, it WAS nothing. Moshay patented the hole. Although Luigi D'Andrea sometimes bought the rights to pick patents held by other inventors, he almost never protected his own ideas, including that of drilling a hole through the center of a pick. Moshay did that himself in 1963. But it wasn't Moshay's hole that changed things for D'Andrea Manufacturing, but his

An assortment of D'Andrea genuine tortoise shell picks from the Golden Age.

argument for putting it there in the first place. According to Moshay, it was to "obviate any tendency for the plectrum to slip out of the grasp of the player." In other words, we were right back to flying picks. The hole was necessary, insisted Moshay, because his pick was made of something even more difficult to grip than celluloid—nylon. And while Moshay's picks themselves would never present a threat to D'Andrea, his material idea caught the eye of one firm that soon would:

Herco, the company that made the nylon pick famous.

The evolution of the nylon pick: The D'Andrea No. 350 pick with a hole in it led to Joseph Moshay's patented nylon pick with a hole, which in turn was the inspiration for the famous Herco nylon pick.

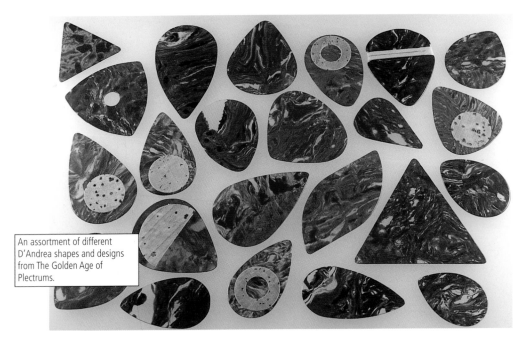

An assortment of different D'Andrea shapes and designs from The Golden Age of Plectrums.

Chapter 5

THE GOLDEN AGE OF PLECTRUMS, 1925-1955

The Golden Age of Plectrums began in the second half of the Roaring Twenties—that complex though fabulous post-World War I period of youthful rebellion and prosperity that broke the moral shackles of the Victorian Era and unleashed both the Jazz Age and the Lawless Decade. It was a time of Prohibition and outrageous excess in which popular music played a crucial role. For every short-skirted, long-legged flapper who danced the Charleston and behaved scandalously in public, there was a ukulele-strumming, coonskin-coat-clad "sheik" ready to light her cigarette. It was all designed to be thoroughly modern. The period was defined by Percy Marks' social commentary *The Plastic Age*.

A few accessories from "The Roaring Twenties," also known as "The Plastic Age."

Stutz Bearcats were the rage. Car radios had entered the American mainstream—as had tube lipstick, pop-up toasters, crossword puzzles, electric razors, jukeboxes, motels and Luigi D'Andrea's full line of stringed instrument plectrums. In their own minute way, picks were a perfect complement for the times. They were accessory, they were colorful and they were plastic. Most of all, they were a piece of the musical phantasmagoria. "Talkies," radio and phonograph records were popularizing instrumental music as never before. Jazz bands featured plectrum-wielding banjo and guitar players. Increasingly, the public fell under the

Below, three very rare plectrums from the 1928 D'Andrea catalog that were not offered in later years: (left to right),Numbers 21A, 26A and 18A.

The distinctive No. 347 pick, center, was one of the widest picks D'Andrea ever made. Left, a No. 347 3/4 pick; right, a No. 347 1/2 pick. Today, the smaller pick has become the No. 347. The two larger sizes are no longer made.

One of the largest D'Andrea picks, a No. 360, left, next to one of the smallest (number unknown). Pick on right is genuine tortoise shell.

influence of plectrum-style guitarists such as Eddie Condon, who in the late '20s hosted basement "jam sessions" in Chicago with the likes of Bix Beiderbecke and Benny Goodman. To be sure, stringed instruments wouldn't approach the popularity they would enjoy in the 1960s. But from a standpoint of quality picks, musicians were given a stunning assortment to chose from between 1925 and 1955.

There were dozens of shapes in patterns swirled and mottled. For mandolins the selection included tiny half-inch ovals and whopping two-inch teardrops, with variations in between. Banjo picks came in a range of wide ovals and big triangles. Practically any shape was

acceptable for the guitar, but predominantly, the preferred guitar plectrum was the one-inch rounded isosceles triangle. In making these plectrums, attention was paid to detail. Often picks were hand-cast with mallet and die and the edges individually beveled with a sander ("unfinished" picks without beveled edges were available at a discount). After the die-casting process became automated, the edges were rounded by running the picks through industrial tumblers mixed with lubricants and abrasives that included volcanic pumice and crushed corncobs. Even then, the inner point edges on deluxe picks used by professionals were often "feathered" by hand, similar to the

Right, D'Andrea No. 336C, and No. 350.

D'Andrea No. 359 pick, center; same shape with a cork ring, left, and cork pad, right.

edges of an airplane prop. Generally, picks of this period came in three gauges, light (.02-inch) medium (.03-inch) and heavy (.04-inch).

The Roaring Twenties crashed and burned with the stock market on October 29, 1929, but stringed instruments and the picks that went with them fared well during the Great Depression. Music provided a form of cheap entertainment as well as a needed morale booster for the impoverished masses. The Grand Ole Opry, which made its radio debut in 1927 and featured stringed instrument virtuosos of every stripe, became more popular when listening to the parlor radio was all many people could afford in the way of amusement. Grateful Americans who tuned in regularly came to regard country performers such as Jimmy

D'Andrea standard No. 351, center; same shape with a cork ring, left, and cork pad, right.

Rodgers and the Carter Family as their own kinfolk. Gene Autry, Roy Rogers and Tex Ritter became western music singing sensations. Woody Guthrie and other Depression-era folk singers made the steel-string guitar a necessary piece of equipment for even a down-and-out balladeer. The U.S government got in on the act by sponsoring thousands of free concerts through the Federal Music Project. Musi-

Two early Martin standard picks. Martin's Golden Age pick selection was small in comparison to Gibson and Gretsch.

cians got an even greater boost during World War II when the government did everything imaginable to keep the troops entertained both at home and abroad. Live radio, which made celebrities of hundreds of regional guitar-strumming troubadours around the nation, was a primary source of entertainment throughout the post-war years.

To supply so many musicians with picks, music dealers turned to a network of jobbers, wholesale mail-order supply houses and instrument companies such as Gibson and

An assortment of Golden Age Gibson picks (the one second from the left is made of genuine tortoise shell).

This five-sided plectrum pictured in a 1932 musical accessories catalog, was made of Galaith, a trade name for the protein plastic, casein, which is made from milk.

No. G-996. Galaith composition Tenor Banjo Pick furnished in assorted colors.

No. 80-L Brown Eddie Lang Pick
Brown celluloid tortoise with laminated white corrugated grip. Medium or heavy.

No. 81-R White Harry Reser Pick
White celluloid tortoise with laminated brown corrugated grip. Light or medium.
Doz. $1.50; Gross $15.00

The Eddie Lang and Harry Reser pick entries from the 1934 Gibson catalog.

Gretsch. (Although the Martin company offered a small selection of picks after 1934, the company never began to seriously market instrument accessories until the mid-1970s.) Gibson, in fact, had offered music instructors and schools a catalog selection of oval picks in celluloid, "fibre" and sole leather prior to World War I. But, by the 1930s, the Gibson line had expanded to include everything from imported genuine tortoise shells to a full line of celluloids and even a colorful five-sided pick made of "Galaith," or casein, a plastic made from the milk of contented moo cows.

Gibson's assortment also listed two of the first celebrity imprint plectrums—the Harry Reser and Eddie Lang picks. Reser was a noted banjo player and Lang a jazz guitarist who had backed up Bing Crosby. Both picks featured a unique design. Reser's, a white oval with a laminated brown corrugated grip, was slightly smaller than Lang's oval, which was the opposite coloring—brown with a laminated white corrugated grip. Celebrity imprints were set to become an industry unto themselves.

Diamond-shape, Bob Clifton Tu-Way pick, circa 1940s.

By the 1940s the names of such noted instrumentalists as Nick Lucas, Nick Manoloff, George Barnes, Les Paul and Roy Smeck were endorsing entire lines of picks. Among the more unusual

Above left, a D'Andrea-made Gretsch medium pick from the Golden Age.

Above right, the "moire grip" pick, from the 1934 Targ & Dinner music catalog, is an example of the fancy picks that were occasionally offered exclusively by some distributors.

Moire grip. Beveled edges.
No. 3515. Dz. **$1.00**
Gross **$10.00**

Above left, a D'Andrea made "grain ivory" crescent grip pick.

Above right, the Gretsch "Non-Skid" Pick may have been the only plectrum that utilized both celluloid and vulcanized rubber (the material used to make the round "Non-Skid" patch).

products of this sort was Bob Clifton's patented Tu-Way Pick, a diamond-shaped plectrum that came in two sizes and assorted colors.

The Gretsch assortment was even more comprehensive than Gibson's and contained several innovations. Gretsch "Non-Skid" celluloid banjo and mandolin picks came in four shapes, three gauges and two color patterns, "Tortoise" and "Ivory." These picks were laminated on each side with a thin patch of hard rubber ridges. They may have been the only plectrums ever produced that combined celluloid and vulcanized rubber. Two other unusual Gretsch picks were a thick celluloid "Ivory" with two points and six sides, and an oversize rounded-square with four points in genuine tortoise shell.

To compete, large instrumental supply houses offered a wide array of plectrums that frequently included one or two styles not generally available elsewhere. These were priced accordingly. For instance, the 1934 catalog of Targ & Dinner, Inc., a music mail-order company out of Chicago, had a "moire grip" celluloid oval, which at $10 a gross was twice the price of a plain celluloid in the same shape. Even more impressive were the company's three-pointed and "crescent grip" picks. The triple pointer looked like a pinwheel while the "crescent grip" was an oval with a small quar-

Two Golden Age D'Andrea No. 355 picks in mosaic or "assorted colors."

Above left, D'Andrea Golden Age No. 348 mosaic.

Above right, D'Andrea Golden Age No. 351 mosaic.

ter-moon strip of celluloid at the rounded, or top edge. Both of these beauties came in assorted colors and sold wholesale for $8 and $13 per gross, respectively.

The mosaic or "assorted color" picks of the era were an example of the extraordinary attributes of celluloid that cannot be duplicated with any other form of plastic to this day (although celluloid's cousin, cellulose acetate, is capable of coming close). Celluloid can be made in a rainbow of opaque, translucent or variegated colors. Moreover, as a thermoplastic material, celluloid can be reheated and reshaped over and over (similar to other

D'Andrea Golden Age No. 346 mosaic.

thermoplastic substances—gold, wax or glass, for instance). Plastics manufacturers took advantage of these properties by ingeniously fusing leftover scraps of crushed celluloid, forming new sheets of breathtaking multi-colored patterns.

Around 1934 Luigi D'Andrea began to tout his "Cushion Grip" pick, which, said his catalog, represented "the only real improvement since picks were made," an overstatement that at least served to emphasize D'Andrea's pride in the design. D'Andrea had "Cushion Grip" trademarked and the shape represented the company's logo. Resembling an Indian arrowhead, the pick itself came in seven size and shape variations and featured small grooves on the sides of each pick around which

Six different D'Andrea Cushion Grip picks. The company made Cushion Grip picks of both celluloid and genuine tortoise shell between the mid-1930s and mid-1940s. Examples of such picks with their original rubber cushions are extremely rare. Those pictured have rubber band substitutes.

Left, Two No. 317G D'Andrea Cushion Grip picks, with and without "cushions." Note the similarity between these picks and an Indian arrowhead.

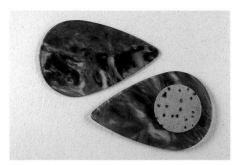

Above, D'Andrea No. 349, top, same shape with a cork pad, bottom.

From left: small mandolin pick (number unknown), No. 363, No. 367 and a 363 shape with a cork ring. All D'Andrea-made in the Golden Age.

Below, clockwise from top left: D'Andrea No. 348 ½, No. 353, No. 354, and No. 358 ½.

a cushion rubber band was fastened. "Cushion Grips" came in both celluloid and tortoise shell. It's possible that D'Andrea created the design to spotlight his new line of genuine tortoise shell picks, which were introduced around the same time. By 1946 "Cushion Grips" were available only in celluloid. All that was left of the "Cushion Grip" pick when the company introduced its 1952-53 catalog was the logo.

Luigi D'Andrea himself had faded to the background in 1953. He died a year later. In his place, the company promised a "new generation of D'Andreas—Anthony and Victor— (who) have pledged themselves to maintain the same high standards established by their well-

The No. 347 pick on the left is made of Japanese celluloid, circa 1970s, while the one on the right is made of Italian celluloid, Golden Age. Both D'Andrea-made.

D'Andrea No. 348, right, and the same pick with a cork pad.

D'Andrea No. 353 shape, left, and No. 354 shape, with cork rings.

known father.... " What Anthony and Victor could not have foreseen, however, was that within two years they would face a challenge that would not only alter the music industry and the pick business forever, but change the fabric of society itself. Those naughty flappers and sheiks of thirty years before, who had so shamelessly shocked their mothers and fathers, were about to encounter a disturbing rebellion instigated by their own ungrateful offspring. It was, they were certain, a phenomenon that could only lead to the ruination of civilization: the advent
of rock 'n' roll.

Right, an unusual mandolin pick of unknown origin, possibly made in the 1940s. Not a D'Andrea shape.

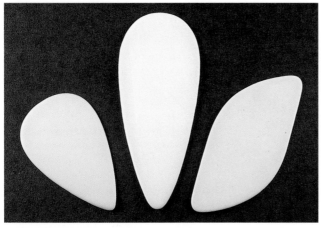

D'Andrea No 355 in white celluloid.

Above, left to right: D'Andrea No. 359, No. 366 and No. 361 in white celluloid.

Below, Two uncommon mandolin pick patterns, origin unknown.

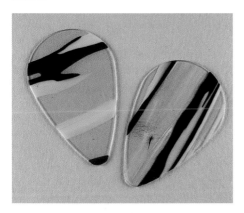

Right, an unusual blue speckled No. 363 $1/2$ mandolin pick.

D'Andrea No. 361. This striking trapezoid is $1/8$ of an inch shy of being a full two inches in length.

An assortment of unusual D'Andrea picks from the 1930s with heart, diamond and spade cork grips.

Below, A D'Andrea heart-shape pick, left, and a very uncommon D'Andrea-made rectangular pick.

Above, two classic mandolin picks from the Golden Age in "grain ivory," left, and "shell." D'Andrea No. 358 ½.

Chapter 6

HAIL, HAIL ROCK 'N' ROLL
AND THE GREAT PICK EXPLOSION

In the summer of 1955 a wave of energy slammed into the earth with all the force of a comet. The impact, as a matter of fact, had been caused in part by a Comet—Danny Cedrone, lead guitarist for Bill Haley's back-up group. "Rock Around the Clock" by Haley and the Comets ascended to the No.1 chart position, where it remained lodged for two full months. The high-speed, frenetic tones Cedrone generated in the song's instrumental ride could only be produced by plucking the steel strings of an amplified electric guitar with a pick. It was something the average teenager hadn't heard before—pure rock 'n' roll. It was enough to send youthful hormones, already raging in the July heat, into hyperdrive and parents into a state of high anxiety. School officials, the clergy, politicians, Clare Booth Luce, *Time* magazine and Frank Sinatra expressed such moral indignation that kids everywhere were left little choice than to embrace the sound with exuberance. What's an adolescent to do in the face of authoritarian outrage? Before the fun posse could head rock 'n' roll off at the pass, Chuck Berry whipped out his guitar and scored a direct Top 10 hit with "Maybellene." That was followed by Carl Perkin's Top 5 smash "Blue Suede Shoes." Then, on January 27, 1956, Elvis Presley released "Heartbreak Hotel," which promptly duplicated "Rock Around the Clock"'s chart-topping position and longevity record. Rock 'n' roll was here to stay.

The sound emitting from so much harmonizing and picking was an interracial marriage of black rhythm and blues and white western swing and country. Heavily influenced by such performers as B.B. King and Muddy Waters, rock 'n' roll featured a distinct $^4/_4$ time signature that put the accent on the second and fourth beats. The effect was both primitive and kinetic and a far cry from the smooth tunes of days gone by that accented the more civilized first and third beats.

One result of the phenomenon was that it placed the six-string guitar, both electric and acoustic, squarely in the limelight of popular music. Previously the Hit Parade had been dominated by stand-up crooners like Perry Como, Rosemary Clooney and Guy Mitchell, who depended on a background orchestra. Overnight they were joined by the likes of Chuck Berry, Bo Diddley and Bill Haley, who were not only backed up by guitars, but who played a guitar themselves. With a single twang, Elvis Presley's guitar practically blew away every other type of fretted stringed instrument that had preceded it. Suddenly, guitar pickers were all over the charts—the Everly Brothers, Duane Eddy, the Ventures, Roy Orbison and Ricky Nelson. And if Ozzie and Harriet's kid—who only knew two chords when he cut his first hit single, "I'm Walkin',"—could do it, any kid could do it. All that was needed was a guitar. And a guitar pick.

Rock 'n' roll marked the beginning of the decline of exotic mandolin and banjo picks and the surge in demand for guitar picks, namely picks of the "standard" or "Lucas" shape. (Rock 'n' roll also effectively killed the term plectrum, an excruciating word containing far too many syllables for the average teenager to

Left, with the coming of rock 'n' roll, picks were increasingly made of plastics other than celluloid. These non-celluloid examples are on a Kay pick guard, which, by contrast, is celluloid.

Right, an early Herco pick from the 1940s. But Herco didn't get into picks in a big way until after rock 'n' roll began.

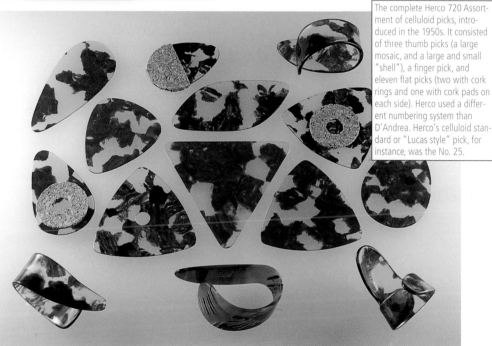

The complete Herco 720 Assortment of celluloid picks, introduced in the 1950s. It consisted of three thumb picks (a large mosaic, and a large and small "shell"), a finger pick, and eleven flat picks (two with cork rings and one with cork pads on each side). Herco used a different numbering system than D'Andrea. Herco's celluloid standard or "Lucas style" pick, for instance, was the No. 25.

Above, "The Adventures of Harry Herco." An ad from the early 1970s.

A box of vintage Herco No. 36 guitar picks and the company's 1966 catalog.

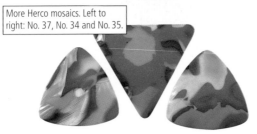

More Herco mosaics. Left to right: No. 37, No. 34 and No. 35.

condone.) Guitar accessories became an important business unto themselves. The D'Andrea company, which up to this point had all but owned the pick-manufacturing game, found itself facing competition. Initially it came from the Hershman Musical Instrument Company of New York, which had been around since 1940. The company's accessory division was called Herco. In the mid-1950s the Hershman brothers, Eddie and Jerry, unveiled Herco's No. 720 assortment of celluloid "guitar picks," which included shapes that previously had been considered mandolin and banjo designs. The 720 line—eleven flat picks and four thumb and finger picks—was made in Japan by the Atsuta family. Japanese manufacturers, who had been dealing in celluloid products in a big way since the end of World War II, were able to duplicate D'Andrea styles so perfectly that few musicians could tell the difference (although D'Andrea and Herco used differing celluloid "tortoise shell" patterns).

The early 1960s saw a second guitar boom with the advent of the folk music movement. The Kingston Trio, the Highwaymen, Peter, Paul & Mary, the Rooftop Singers and other groups were producing one chart buster after another.

"Enlightened" baby boomers, who were coming of age, began turning to the folksy,

Above, Herco celluloid mosaics. Left to right: No. 20, No. 25 and No. 29. These stunning picks were only made when supplies of Herco's regular "shell" celluloid were unavailable. The company instructed the Japanese manufacturer to stop making Herco picks in "assorted colors" (the one exception was the large mosaic thumb pick).

Below, the pick on the left is not a Herco pick, although the mosaic celluloid appears to be identical to that used in the Herco No. 15, center, and No. 30, right.

Above, four examples of the dazzling celluloid mosaic picks that were made in Japan after the 1960s. These are not Herco picks.

politically charged lyrics of guitar-playing balladeers like Joan Baez, Phil Ochs and Bob Dylan. In the mid-1960s scarcely a college dorm in America didn't house at least one troubadour who knew every verse of "A Hard Rain's A-Gonna Fall." Dylan's folk rock expansion only added a new dimension to the frenzy. Then, in 1964, Liverpool invaded the country via the Beatles, and, according to Jerry Hershman, "You could sell anything that even resembled a guitar pick."

To deal with that kind of demand, Herco began the search to find a substitute for celluloid, which was volatile, increasingly scarce and time-consuming to produce. When the company took a squint at Joe Moshay's nylon pick with a hole in it, it felt the answer had been found. Not only is nylon more durable than celluloid, but it can be both injection-molded or extruded into sheets for die cutting.

And, if it lacked the raw beauty and tone purity of celluloid, the fans didn't seem to mind so long as it was marketed properly. And market nylon picks Herco did.

Herco introduced two nylon picks, a light-gauge Gold and a heavy-gauge Silver, which sold for 25 cents each. Both picks were the "Lucas" shape and employed a no-nonsense crosshatch grip design. To accommodate a growing lower-end market, in 1966 the com-

Above, Herco's "Ghastly Green" economy line of "Flexylon" (nylon) picks. Clockwise from the top, No. 409, No. 405, No. 403, No. 401 and No. 407. Dealer price was $4.50 for three dozen.

Below, Herco's famous nylon guitar pick. Left, the No. 211 silver heavy gauge Flex 75, and, right, the No. 210 gold light gauge Flex 50. Dealer price was $7.20 for three dozen.

Left, a Herco No. 25; right, a D'Andrea No. 351.

Above left, a Herco No. 44; right, a D'Andrea No. 336C. Note the difference in celluloid patterns and cork textures.

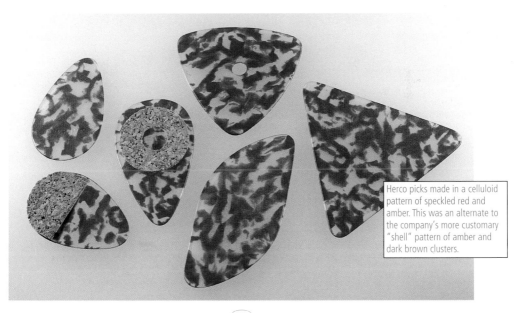

Herco picks made in a celluloid pattern of speckled red and amber. This was an alternate to the company's more customary "shell" pattern of amber and dark brown clusters.

Left, a Herco No. 36; right, a D'Andrea No. 337C.

Three Herco No. 30 picks showing various celluloid color patterns. The pattern on the right was commonly used by D'Andrea, and almost never used by Herco.

Above, the John Pearse "Studio" pick, left, beside a mirror image, corrugated Japan-made Yamaha pick. Pearse's pick patent applied to the United States only.

Right, the evolution of a John Pearse pick. Left, the musician and pick inventor's original, 1975 "Broken Heart" pick prototype, featuring three different points. Next, the pick as it was finally patented by the Martin Company in 1978. Pearse continued the evolution in 1979 with his "Underdog" pick, which eventually led to his patented "Studio" pick, right, which combines the best qualities of a No. 351 and No. 352 pick, bottom center. The pick is designed to be used for either lead or rhythm guitar.

While some pick companies experimented with different plastics materials in the 1960s, '70s and '80s, D'Andrea, the world's largest pick maker, continued to focus on celluloid. This "Bull's-Eye Professional Pick" card is from the 1970s.

pany announced its "Flexylon" pick assortment, five shapes in "Ghastly Green" that were made of a "new durable material that will not break, chip or peel," and cost from a dime to 15 cents each. What was this revolutionary new substance? The very same nylon used to make the 25-cent picks.

The D'Andrea company remained committed to celluloid. At a time when the American supply of celluloid was drying up, the company had no trouble importing all it needed from Europe. Having been at the pick-making trade longer than anybody, D'Andrea enjoyed an advantage in experience, material resources and manufacturing capabilities. As Herco's Jerry Hershman put it, "When we say we sold a million picks, that was nothing. D'Andrea

was REALLY going crazy." The Golden Age of Plectrums may have been over, but the Guitar Pick Era was just beginning. And D'Andrea, the company that invented the guitar pick, wasn't about to miss out. While D'Andrea began phasing out many of its wild mandolin and banjo shapes, it also re-standardized its own thickness gauges. Realizing he could get a higher yield for the cost, Anthony D'Andrea shaved his thin-, medium- and heavy-gauge celluloid sheets by .002 inch each, making them .018-inch, .028-inch and .038-inch respectively. Translated into millimeters, the change equalled the ".46mm," ".71mm" and ".96mm" that have identified the gauge imprints on celluloid picks ever since. (In the 1970s, Anthony's son, Tony—an erstwhile rock musi-

Above, a genuine tortoise shell standard pick made in Japan, possibly by Pick Boy, prior to the international ban on such products in the mid-1970s.

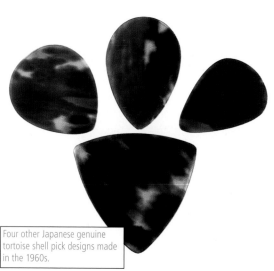

Four other Japanese genuine tortoise shell pick designs made in the 1960s.

cian—joined the company and introduced three additional celluloid gauges: .58mm, .84mm and 1.21mm.)

Meanwhile, back in Japan, Shoji Nakano was orchestrating a pick revolution of his own that would one day touch America. Like Luigi D'Andrea, Nakano stumbled into the pick biz by happenstance, having started out as a dealer in gentlemen's accessory items. One day in 1961, Nakano paid a visit to the factory that produced his tortoise shell shoe horns and became fascinated by a batch of small triangles made from leftover shell scraps. These, he was informed, were "pick fingernails" used to pluck stringed instruments. Intrigued, Nakano—a 36-year-old tinkerer who obviously had an acute sense of timing—bought 20,000 pieces of shell scrap and set up shop. His hunch that there was money to be made in instrumental "fingernails" proved correct beyond his fantasies. In time his operation exploited the growing Japanese guitar market, which was clamoring for picks. Like pick makers before him who came to understand the limitations of tortoise shell, Nakano turned to celluloid. His product line included the usual triangles, ovals and teardrops as well as the "standard" guitar shape. A pick that cost him 3 to 4 yen to produce could be sold for many times that much.

A standard heavy gauge celluloid Pick Boy pick. In the early 1990s, the company cut back its production of celluloid product.

Above, Pick Boy celluloid picks.

Below, four celluloid Jim Dunlop USA picks made in the 1980s, before the company phased out its production of picks made of the first plastic.

By his own account interest in picks during this period "was phenomenal . . . I just couldn't believe how profitable it was." So much so, he later remarked, "I kind of feel bad about it."

At the height of production in the early 1970s, Nakano was turning out 700,000 picks a month. By the end of the decade he had expanded his operation to Frankfurt, Germany, and devised a catchy new moniker for his company: Pick Boy. The company would go on to become one of the three largest pick companies in the world.

But the ride wouldn't be as easy as Danny Cedrone's nimble riff on the recording that launched rock 'n' roll. Looming on the horizon was Jim Dunlop, a Scot marketing genius who would turn a single capo idea into a guitar accessory and pick empire that would one day rival D'Andrea and Pick Boy and swallow Herco alive. By the late 1970s "the party was over" anyhow, in the words of Jerry Hershman. Guitar sales in America, which had soared from 1955 through the '60s, peaked at 2,200,000 in 1970 and began a nosedive. By 1983 the figure was down to 875,000. The pick bubble popped as well. The reasons were multiple and had to do with changing music and lifestyles. Primarily, they had to do with the baby boomers who created the great pick explosion in the first place. To the relief of their parents, most survived rock 'n' roll, the '60s and the Age of Aquarius and were ready to become responsible enough adults to detest whatever music their own offspring would embrace. Finally, they had embarked on their working careers and were forced to lay the implements of their youth in the closet.

But picks and all that goes with them were hardly finished. The rascals were only waiting for the moment to renew themselves. And when that time arrived, they would make a sound heard all around the world.

Left, standard picks from Pick Boy, circa early 1990s.

A wood-grain standard celluloid pick from D'Andrea, circa 1980s.

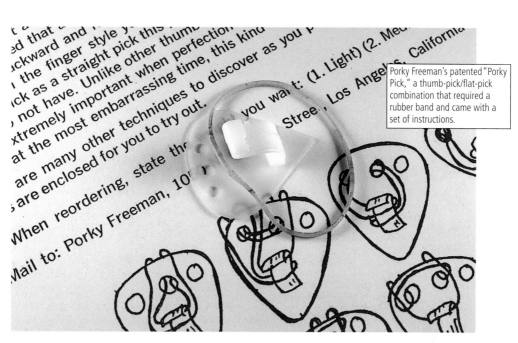

Porky Freeman's patented "Porky Pick," a thumb-pick/flat-pick combination that required a rubber band and came with a set of instructions.

Chapter 7

COLLECTING PICKS

In a society with a propensity to hoard every conceivable object—from advertising tins to zoot suits—it is remarkable that fretted stringed instrument plectrums managed to fall through the cracks. But then, picks always were small and thin. Ironically, because they were overlooked for so long, they offer a rare and appealing opportunity in the realm of collectibles. Picks are cheap, hundreds can be stored in a single sandwich bag and, particularly in the case of those made of celluloid, they are often magnificent. Millions were produced during the 20th century in an ample array of materials and designs. New picks, of course, can be bought at any music store or through instrument

Two examples of weird imprints that might form the foundation of a pick collection.

Pick collector Harry Anderson, Jr. of La Mirada, California, with a small sample of his collection of picks from every state.

mail order catalogs. Where to find the old variety is more scavenger hunt than science. They could be anywhere. No doubt thousands reside exactly where they were last tossed, in bureau drawers, cigar boxes or dusty banjo cases stuffed in dark and forgotten closets. One place to start is the most obvious—old music shops, which often have remnants from the romance days still rattling around behind the counter. Vintage guitar emporiums, repair shops, luthiers, pawn dealers and antique establishments are other locations to consider. Picks are hiding out there in large numbers. Many are merely waiting to be rediscovered.

Which is not to say there were never those who kept a stash of picks. Celebrity imprint picks were gathered up by scattered rock fans back in the 1970s and probably before that. In July of 1975 *Guitar Player* magazine piqued pick curiosity with an article by Steve Rosen that featured picks touched by the fingers of such immortals as Jimi Hendrix, Eric Clapton and John McLaughlin. Still, collecting these instrument accessories remained more a matter of individual whimsy than anything else. Before the late 1980s, there was no semblance of a structured collectible pick market in America. Soon, though, there were indications that picks were at least beginning to be appreciated as an entity unto themselves. Classified

This assortment of different Fender picks is only a fraction of the different Fender designs that have been made. Except for the bottom right pick, made of an acetal polymer industrial plastic known as Delrin, these are all celluloids.

ads for picks sprang up in music publications and a small network of collectors from around the country began buying and trading among themselves. Paul Hettinger of Winamac, Indiana, amassed in excess of 4,000 celebrity imprints, including dozens of different Van Halen picks. Harry Anderson, Jr. of La Mirada, California, began showing up at West Coast guitar fairs and exhibitions with his own impressive collection, which contained imprints from nearly every state. Guitar picks, as well as banjo and mandolin plectrums, had reached the first stage of becoming genuine collectible items in their own right.

As with most things collectible, anyone who wants to begin a pick collection should target a category. The possibilities are myriad. Celebrity rock and country imprints are an obvious choice. A collection of every Fender pick ever marketed would be fascinating as well. Or, picks could be collected by material—

Above, an unusual Nick Lucas pick card distributed by the Grover Musical Products company, possibly in the 1960s. This card is different than the Nick Lucas "Pick with The Crooning Tone" cards that were so familiar in the 1930s, '40s and '50s.

Above right, a Grover Deluxe Nick Lucas pick card. Like virtually all Nick Lucas celluloid picks, these were made by D'Andrea.

stone, metal, wood, tortoise shell, etc. One could accumulate promotional imprints or maintain a subcategory collection of oddball imprints, such as "Purloined from McCabe's," or, "Life Is Short Play Loud." Accumulators of the weird could focus on bizarre picks, like Luke Hart's riveted, five-layer, double-cross plectrum, or Porky Freeman's patented "Porky Pick," a rubber band and flat-pick/thumb-pick combination that was so complicated it came with a ten-point set of instructions. Yet another possibility would be to compile colorful retail pick cards carried in music shops throughout the 1930s, '40s and '50s. These cardboard displays generally contained two dozen picks at 10 cents each, three for a quarter. Name brands associated with cards included Nick Lucas, Nick Manoloff, Bob Clifton, George Barnes, Les Paul, Wabash, Fender, Gibson, D'Andrea, Guild, Cole's (felt ukulele picks) and Premier (genuine tortoise shell).

Possibly the least-tapped and most intriguing area of pick collecting is vintage celluloid picks from The Golden Age of Plectrums. But this period—1925 through 1955—should be considered in general terms. It begins roughly around the time Luigi D'Andrea introduced his spectacular assortment of celluloid picks, and ends with the advent of rock 'n' roll. The era marks a generation when there was a burst of pick styles available for guitars, mandolins and banjos. Following "Rock Around the Clock," the instrumental emphasis shifted directly to guitars. In so doing, fewer pick shapes were marketed and many of the older designs were discontinued.

Certainly, however, there were wonderful picks around before and after that period. Examples from the pioneers—Charles F.W. Seidel's multi-point plectrum or Aaron Burdwise's wire loop pick—would be prized vintage collectibles. Likewise, some exquisite picks were marketed after 1955. Herco's No. 720

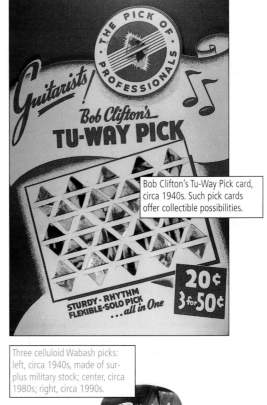

Bob Clifton's Tu-Way Pick card, circa 1940s. Such pick cards offer collectible possibilities.

Three celluloid Wabash picks: left, circa 1940s, made of surplus military stock; center, circa 1980s; right, circa 1990s.

This Grover medium Nick Lucas pick carried the guitarist's familiar, stylized imprint.

Above, the Grover Deluxe Nick Lucas pick, made by D'Andrea, is a bit of an oddity in that it's not the standard "Lucas shape"— but a combination of the No. 348, left, and No. 351, right.

assortment is a prime example. Beginning in the late 1950s the company ordered these Japan-made picks in two celluloid "tortoise shell" patterns. On a few occasions, apparently when the makers had exhausted their supply of appropriate patterns, the picks arrived in vivid assorted colors. Chagrined because its promotional material did not mention assorted flatpick colors, the company instructed the Japanese manufacturers to refrain. As a conse–quence, Herco's mosaic celluloids have become as desirable as they are difficult to find.

Otherwise, Herco's No. 720 Assortment consisted of picks that were almost identical to designs and shapes made by D'Andrea, and even incorporated D'Andrea-like cork rings and pads. Nevertheless, Herco and D'Andrea celluloids can be distinguished from one another in several ways. First, D'Andrea and

Herco used different "tortoise shell" patterns. D'Andrea's most common pattern was a distinctive mass of tight, fluid, reddish-brown swirls. This pattern was almost never used by Herco. Herco's usual pattern appeared as clusters of larger, abstract configurations in contrasting hues of dark brown and amber. Herco celluloids also came in a speckled red and amber pattern (on occasion D'Andrea also used this pattern). In addition to celluloid patterns, each company used a different type of cork. Herco's was the coarser of the two, and the company's rings and pads were slightly thicker than the smooth rings and pads found on D'Andrea picks. Finally, every Herco celluloid pick carried a "Japan" imprint. The lettering was usually so tiny that few musicians noticed. But through an ordinary magnifying glass the imprint is discernible, provided it hasn't been worn away by time and usage.

Virtually any pick from the Golden Age is collectible. Those that can be included among the exceptional:

*Nick Lucas. Since the Nick Lucas shape became the "standard" guitar pick, the Lucas pick has the added distinction of being the first guitar pick with an imprint. Although Lucas celluloid picks were made for years, they were never made in enormous numbers, such as were Fender picks.

*Lang and Reser. Eddie Lang and Harry Reser were two noted instrumentalists of the 1920s and '30s who were among the first to have stylized imprints. Both picks were unusual in that they were laminated as well as corrugated.

*McNeil. Charles McNeil was another early instrumentalist and songwriter who, in the 1930s, devised one of the first plectrum guitar courses, the "McNeil Modern Method." The McNeil imprint pick was an oval with corrugations that were distinctive because they were irregular and obviously handmade.

A 1961 Giuseppe Pettine mandolin pick ad. For decades D'Andrea made Pettine picks. However, Pettine picks were around before D'Andrea began operations in 1922—possibly they were manufactured in Europe. Today, Pettine picks are hard to find.

*Pettine. Giuseppe Pettine, a noted mandolin player and teacher, operated the Rhode Island Music Co. of Providence. Pettine plectrums were teardrop-shaped and date as far back as 1910. Probably first made in Europe, they were later manufactured by D'Andrea and nearly always carried the Pettine imprint. Pettine picks eventually included the Lucas shape, and were available until the 1970s, probably a longevity record among picks.

*Kork Grip. These quality, patented plectrums came in three oval sizes and were popular among professional musicians of the era. Like other deluxe plectrums, Kork Grips had "feathered" or hand-beveled inner edges, a

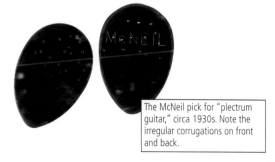

The McNeil pick for "plectrum guitar," circa 1930s. Note the irregular corrugations on front and back.

By the 1970s, demand for the standard cork grip picks, left, had dwindled to such an extent that the extra time and expense in making them no longer justified the effort. In order to placate musicians who still preferred cork grip picks, for a time D'Andrea toyed with simply imprinting a cork ring on a pick, right. Today, cork grip picks are rare; imprinted cork grip picks are extremely rare.

time-consuming feature that disappeared after pick edges were routinely beveled by machine tumblers.

*D'Andrea cork grip. For decades D'Andrea made a wide variety of cork-grip plectrums. Once ubiquitous, in the years after the company discontinued its cork line, they became scarce.

*Cushion Grip. Once the pride of D'Andrea Manufacturing, Cushion Grip picks were only made in the 1930s and '40s. They came in seven shapes. Like most other picks of the era, they have become hard to find—especially with their original rubber bands intact.

*Crescent Grip. These fascinating ovals featured a small strip of laminated celluloid at the top of the pick that was a different color than the rest of the plectrum. Hen's teeth are easier to find.

*Gretsch "Non-Skid." One of several desirable Gretsch picks, "Non-Skids" promised never to leave one's fingers. Similar in design to a line of deluxe D'Andrea cork pad picks,

Above, although difficult to find, D'Andrea "Crescent Grip" picks—made between the mid-1930s and mid-1940s—can still be located, sometimes in old mandolin cases.

A large "unfinished" mandolin pick; origin unknown, but most likely from the Golden Age.

"Non-Skid" picks came in four shapes, two patterns (shell and ivory), and had a round patch of ribbed hard rubber attached to each side.

*Gibson. Gibson picks are distinctive because many were made before D'Andrea went into business in 1922. These pre-World War I Gibsons may have been manufactured in Europe. It appears that some foreign designs were continued after D'Andrea established an American pick market.

*Unfinished. Like corrugated picks (with patterns of small gripping indentations), unfinished picks were once common. Sold at a discount, they were recognizable by their rough, unbeveled edges. An unfinished celluloid pick is nearly always from the 1930s or before. Later, most picks underwent the automatic deburring process.

Precise dating of vintage celluloid picks is next to impossible in many instances. The picks themselves were never dated, and frequently the same celluloid patterns and die shapes were used year after year. Manufacturing records, which would be helpful, were frequently lost or discarded. It must be remembered that a stringed instrument plectrum was once such a periphery item that insuring its provenance would have seemed absurd. As Tony D'Andrea put it, "No one thought picks would be part of history." Still, by comparing a

Above left, a seldom seen D'Andrea No. 367 1/2 pick.

Above right, an unusual rounded-triangle cork grip pick, probably from the Golden Age. Origin unknown. Not D'Andrea-made.

pick with available catalog information from the period, it's possible to get an idea of its background. Pick shape Numbers 18A and 21A from the 1928 D'Andrea selection, for example, are not to be found in any of the company's subsequent offerings (see Appendix C). It is reasonable to assume, then, that these two mandolin plectrums were only made in the 1920s, and probably only in the mid-to-late '20s at that.

The largest selection of celluloid picks D'Andrea ever offered appeared in the company's 1946-47 listing. By that time the company had long since changed its original numbering system, but most of the familiar shapes were still around. Some, though, had been dropped and new ones added. Used in conjunc-

Above, the maestro of strange picks was the late Luke Hart. This five-layer, riveted, double-cross model ranks as one of the all-time unusual celluloid plectrums. Circa early 1980s.

Below, three more Luke Hart picks: left, a three-layer, riveted thumb pick; center, five-layer, riveted, single-cross pick and, right, a standard flat pick with a protruding wedge. Circa early 1980s.

Above, D'Andrea Golden Age plectrums are not only miniature works of art, they can make fascinating collectibles. Pictured are three classics: No. 352, center; same shape with a cork ring, left, and cork pad, right.

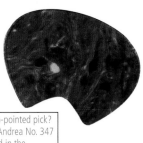

An incredible two-pointed pick? Actually, it's a D'Andrea No. 347 that got mutilated in the automatic die stamping process—in this case, with spectacular results.

tion with one another, the 1928 and 1946-47 catalogs form a sort of Rosetta Stone of vintage celluloid picks from the Golden Age. Although they are by no means complete, the two listings include a high percentage of all the plectrum designs on the market in America from 1925 to 1955 (See Appendix C).

The ultimate vintage pick collection? If one were to dream, it would undoubtedly be to acquire the entire D'Andrea line from the Golden Age of Celluloid Plectrums—every shape in every gauge, and each example in mint condition.

Impossible? It would seem. Certainly nothing approaching such a collection exists as of this writing. Not by any individual nor by the D'Andrea company itself. It is safe to assume that there are no known examples of some early D'Andrea picks in any gauge or condition. To build a complete collection, even if possible, could require years of searching and extraordinary efforts. Then again, who's been looking all that hard? And, in a society with a propensity to hoard every conceivable object, more amazing things have been known to happen.

Above, three unusual modern picks: left, the "Triplet" pick; center, the "McPherson Studio Design;" and the colossal 8-prong "Strum Rose" pick.

Below, more peculiar picks: left, an environmentally correct pick made of recycled plastics; center, a battery-operated "Tric Pick" that lights up in the dark; and a "Fender" pick.

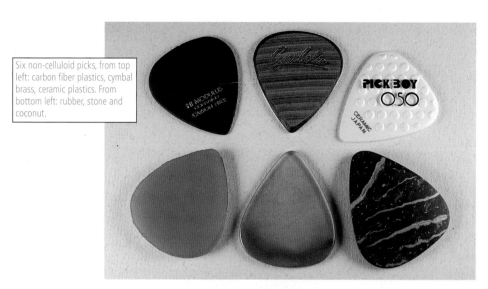

Six non-celluloid picks, from top left: carbon fiber plastics, cymbal brass, ceramic plastics. From bottom left: rubber, stone and coconut.

Other than celluloid, modern picks are made of a number of different synthetic materials, including nylon, acetal polymer, composite and laminated plastics. Pictured here are several non-celluloid picks from Dunlop USA.

Above left, LePik, made of nylon-like "Fibylon," and a nylon Segovia pick with hard, soft and medium points.

Above right, three color-coded picks from Martin, circa 1980s. Red, light; white, medium; and blue, hard. By the 1990s, Martin no longer color coded these picks, but offered them in one color, amber, and in light, medium and hard gauges. Not celluloid.

Left, an assortment of metal picks made of steel, brass and bronze.

An agate pick.

A collection of commercial imprint picks.

Three impressive "Coast" imprint picks.

Vintage Epiphone pick, circa early 1970s.

Matches, needles and emery boards can be used to determine if a pick is really celluloid. In this case, the best method is simply to look at it. If it's translucent and multi-colored, most likely it's celluloid (or genuine tortoise shell).

Chapter 8

THE CARE AND FEEDING OF A VINTAGE CELLULOID PLECTRUM

Before a celluloid plectrum can be properly attended to, it must first be distinguished from a pick made of any other type of plastic. There is one absolutely foolproof way to do this: holding the pick firmly with a pair of tweezers or similar pincer, carefully touch it to a flame. If the pick ignites instantly, burns ferociously for eight seconds and poofs out, leaving nothing but a whiff of smoky mothballs, it is 100 percent certain the pick was celluloid.

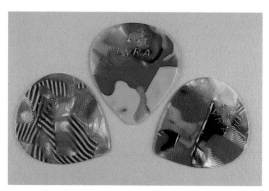

These impressive made-in-Japan Lyra picks, circa early 1980s, are sure to be celluloid since they are mosaic or "assorted colors."

Left, a D'Andrea No. 46 cork grip as seen in the company's 1928 catalog. Right, a D'Andrea No. 333C cork grip, circa 1946. Basically the same pick, but notice the subtle design differences. Because of their age, these two picks must be either celluloid or genuine tortoise shell. And since D'Andrea never made genuine tortoise shell cork grip picks, it can be assumed that both picks are celluloid.

Celluloid can mimic the look, feel and musical tone quality of a genuine tortoise shell pick. Can you tell which of these four are the genuine article? Answer: the two on the left.

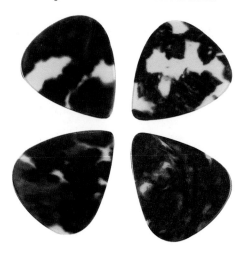

Regrettably, the pick will also be 100 percent missing. Those willing to accept a lesser degree of certainty have other ways to discern celluloid—ways that won't disintegrate a plectrum. If, for instance, the pick is a translucent "tortoise shell" pattern, it is sure to be celluloid, since the only other realistic possibility would be that it's made of genuine tortoise shell. (There are ways to differentiate between celluloid and genuine tortoise shell, too. The surface of a celluloid pick is uniform and has a semi-matte finish, while that of a tortoise shell pick is usually glossy and displays telltale wavy lines. Celluloid picks have a dull, flat sound when dropped on a table or countertop;

real tortoise shells have more bounce and emit a crisp, tonal sound.) If a pick has a "tortoise shell" pattern and is shaped like any of the more unusual styles from the Golden Age of Plectrums, there's a 90 percent-plus chance that it is celluloid.

If a collector is still in doubt, the time has come to release the camphor vapors—that mothball scent commonly associated with celluloid. How to do that without destroying the pick will be explained. For now, the point is this: if the pick does release camphor vapors, there's a 99.99 percent chance that it's celluloid. Anyone preoccupied with that .01 percent of a doubt is probably less of a pick collector than a pyromaniac.

To recap then—if a plastic pick looks like tortoise shell, the odds are overwhelming that it's celluloid—especially if it's an old and odd shape. No further testing is necessary. This same rule applies to picks with assorted or mosaic colors. If, on the other hand, the pick is a common shape and has an opaque, solid color, the camphor vapors must be released to be positive it's celluloid.

Natural camphor is the characteristic white resin of an Asian lauraceous tree and is used in disinfectants, counterirritants and, not surprisingly, mothballs. It is also the magic solvent John Wesley Hyatt combined with

In this photo, the characteristic ripple or wavy effect of a genuine tortoise shell pick can be seen in the bottom left plectrum. The pick on the bottom right is a rare, "unfinished" genuine tortoise shell pick.

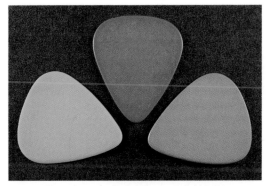

Opaque picks can be made of celluloid or non-celluloid plastics. These three are made of Delrin.

These two unusual heart-shape picks, while not translucent, have that distinctive celluloid look and feel.

cellulose nitrate to create celluloid. Collectors of antique celluloid objects know all about camphor and have devised a number of unscientific procedures for releasing its distinct odor—none of which always work (as we learned in Chapter 2, celluloid is nothing if not unpredictable). One approach is to rub the object, in this case a pick, vigorously across one's clothing. Frictional heat will frequently release the identifying fumes. The same thing can sometimes be achieved by holding the pick between the thumb and index finger and firmly rubbing it with the thumb. However, because frictional methods could damage a pick (particularly one with an aging, fragile cork ring or pad), such tests are not recommended.

Another idea is the taste test. A celluloid pick will usually leave a camphor taste—a mild, tingly menthol essence—on the tongue.

The easiest way for one to become familiar with it is to wash a "tortoise shell" Fender pick and then suck on it for a moment. Any other pick with a similar taste is celluloid. This epicurean approach is also not recommended.

Yet another trick is to heat a needle point over a flame and pierce an obscure part of the plastic object. If the point sinks in easily and the scent of camphor prevails, the object is celluloid. Since there are generally no obscure parts to a pick, this method is almost never a good idea for celluloid plectrum detection.

The recommended way to test a pick is to gently scrape the fine, softer side of an ordinary emery board across the edge of the plectrum. The effects of the emery board are not noticeable and more often than not, if the pick is celluloid, the camphor vapors will be instantly apparent.

Once it has been established that a pick is celluloid, it is advisable to begin treating it appropriately. Celluloid picks, particularly the vintage variety, need special care. Ironically, this is in part because celluloid is not, and never has been, a "cheap plastic."

Manufacturing celluloid requires large, expensive equipment. Once it has been made, celluloid takes weeks or months to cure before it can be sliced into sheets. The plastic begins as a cool, dough-like material that can be treated with all manner of dyes and pigments. This unique aspect of celluloid is the secret to the striking array of designs it can produce. "Tortoise shell" patterns were produced by delicately adding aniline dyes to the otherwise clear plastic as it hardened. All this art was so wonderful no one paid attention to the implications of how these dyes and pigments might one day affect the plastic. And, because celluloid was the first commercial plastic, the idea of adding stabilizers, a routine practice in the modern plastics industry, did not occur to early celluloid manufacturers. As a result, decades later the stuff of dreams can become the stuff of nightmares. No one really knows what awful secrets linger within old celluloid walls. But when such objects occasionally decide to rot, warp or crumble, the outcome is never a thing of beauty.

Which doesn't mean there is need to be overly alarmed about vintage celluloid picks. Most are relatively stable in spite of their upbringing, and, if treated properly, should remain intact for decades to come. The first consideration should be whether to actually use such a pick or simply admire it. This depends on individual tastes. However, considering that new picks are readily available for less than a dollar each, it makes little sense to risk damaging a vintage plectrum. Still, if one

These modern Pro Plec picks from D'Andrea are made of a thermoplastic cellulosic material especially designed for picks.

feels a sense of artistic purity by jamming with a pick from the days of Nick Lucas or Les Paul, then so be it. A vintage pick will probably function as well today as it did when it came off the assembly line. But like old cars and grandmas, vintage picks can be fragile and should be accorded due respect.

That includes keeping them out of direct sunlight, which, because of ultraviolet rays, can turn a pick brittle, fade its colors and otherwise hasten its demise. Bright lights and extended exposure to fluorescent lamps should also be avoided. It goes without saying that picks have no business playing with matches or being anywhere near fire. Sparks can be equally devastating. Reports of spontaneous celluloid combustion are true and in many instances the villain has been static electricity. Celluloid picks sometimes don't tolerate extreme changes well—heat and cold, dry or moist atmosphere, and so forth.

Ideally, they should be stored in a cool, dry, dark place (this is why they are often able to emerge in fine condition after decades of confinement in old mandolin cases). Ventilation is always a good idea. It is OK to keep picks sealed in plastic bags and containers, provided they are aired out regularly. A word of caution, however. Celluloid picks apparently adhere to the "one-rotten-apple" rule. In other words, a bad pick can corrupt and degrade those around it. It is safe to display picks in plastic sheets used to mount coins or photo slides. It is preferable to use the more expensive archival quality pages made from inert polypropylene or polyethylene (as opposed to cheaper polyvinyl chloride sheets that could leave an oily film that might adversely affect a pick). These can be ordered from archival supply companies such as Light Impressions of Rochester, New York (see Appendix B). There are also plastic polishes on the market that can be used to restore the luster of a celluloid pick. Novus, Inc. of Minneapolis, Minnesota, sells a No. 2 Plastic Polish, designed to remove fine scratches, that works well on celluloid (see Appendix B).

Repairing a cracked celluloid pick or undoing the effects of one in the throes of turning ugly can be a tricky proposition. Carefully coating a cracked pick with nitrocellulose lacquer can prevent the crack from spreading. Botch the job, and the cure is more unsightly than the crack. Where does one find nitrocellulose lacquer? At any drugstore. It's called clear nail polish (just be sure "nitrocellulose" is mentioned somewhere in the fine print). If a pick is rapidly deteriorating and extreme measures are called for, one collector's guide suggests that soaking it in a bath of baking soda and water for up to three weeks will have a stabilizing effect. After rinsing a soaked pick, it can be safely buffed with plastic polish, or (if the collector has a steady hand and iron nerves), coated with clear nail polish.

If all else fails, one can resort to subjecting the pick to the ultimate celluloid test. If a vintage celluloid plectrum must die, it is better that it should go out in an eight-second blaze of glory.

A mess of celebrity imprint picks.

Chapter 9

PROMOTIONAL PICKS— GET 'EM WHILE THEY'RE HOT!

On a sultry summer evening in 1992 a deal was going down in the back streets of Miami. A sweaty, long-haired male clad in dark attire and snakeskin boots leaned against a large van and nervously puffed a cigarette. Soon, a second figure emerged like a silhouette from the far end of the alley and stepped toward the van.

"You got the stuff?" asked the second figure as he approached.

A rare and potentially valuable Bob Dylan pick.

The opposite side "punch line" of the humorous Dylan pick. Since this pick came from a Dylan roadie, it would be considered authentic by most imprint collectors.

"Yeah," said the first, flipping his cigarette butt to the pavement in a splash of sparks. "You got the money?"

The intruder fished a wad of loot from his jeans and handed it over. After a quick cash count, the van was unlocked and a one-pound bag was withdrawn and tossed to the buyer.

Had the cops swooped down just then with guns drawn and lights flashing, they'd have had a hard time making a case that would stick in court. Inside the pouch they would have found nothing more illegal than promotional guitar picks used by a well-known heavy-metal group, for which the guy in dark garb was the roadie. In one fashion or another this scene was being played out in Los Angeles, Chicago, Atlanta, New York and other major metropoli-

tan areas where, in some quarters, imprinted guitar picks were as precious as drugs.

Why? Because an increasing number of pick collectors around the country were forking over anywhere from $3 to $75 for a one-inch plastic guitar pick that cost pennies to produce. Not just any pick, mind you, but one bearing the name or logo of a recognized act, such as Eric Clapton, Frank Zappa or former Stray Cat, Brian Setzer. Typically, these picks were selling in the $5 to $15 range—Billy Idol, Richie Sambora or Bruce Kulick, for instance. Ace Frehley, Bob Dylan and Keith Richards cost extra due to their scarcity. In a few cases the prices were all out of proportion to the intrinsic value of the object at hand—which, under normal circumstances, would retail for about a half dollar. Paul McCartney promo picks were going for around $100 apiece, a coveted Elvis pick could be had for up to $1,000.

For those "holding" the right picks the profit potential must have seemed staggering. A loose network of buyers, traders and sellers emerged. Road managers were selling picks to dealers who in turn hawked them to collectors. It was a laissez-faire conglomeration in the sense that the dealings were strictly unregulated (few Americans were aware any of this

Left to right: Pat Metheny, Steve Vai (not celluloid), and Carl Wilson.

Left to right: Slash, Billy Joel and Brad Whitford.

was happening). Like much associated with rock 'n' roll, the finagling could be heady stuff. The '90s breed of pick collector gained a reputation for being relentless. Late-night hotel room wrangling, long-distance phone calls at all hours, exorbitant offers for a single pick were routine.

Collectors knew what they wanted: mint-condition celebrity imprints of high-profile guitarists or groups—preferably rock or heavy metal, although country pick collectors were on the rise. Ironically, these same collectors were less inclined to want a non-imprint pick that might have actually been held by a particular artist. A Fender medium used in a recording session by, say, George Harrison, would not command the respect of a Harrison imprint that the guitarist may have never

touched. Provided, of course, the promotional pick was ordered by Harrison himself or one of his crew. Otherwise, the pick would be considered a "fake."

Pick accumulators had been around since the early 1980s or before, although in less radical form. Most often they were fans who hung out by the concert stage in hopes of pilfering whatever pick might land in their laps (increasingly, guitarists fed the frenzy by tossing picks to the crowd). Some collectors, such as Mike Lowe of Forest Park, Illinois, devised a modified strategy. Around 1982 Lowe began handing pickers self-addressed, stamped return envelopes. Many responded. A decade later, Lowe had around 1,200 different imprints—the majority of which he had paid little or nothing to own. But for a new genera-

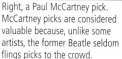

Left, a pick from the legendary R&B artist, B.B. King.

Right, a Paul McCartney pick. McCartney picks are considered valuable because, unlike some artists, the former Beatle seldom flings picks to the crowd.

Could this have been Jimi's actual pick? Even if it were, it wouldn't have much appeal to many celebrity imprint collectors, who'd rather own a genuine "Jimi" pick, even if the legendary musician had never touched it. Unfortunately, it appears that no genuine "Jimi" picks were ever made.

tion of pick grubbers, hell-bent on acquiring a sterling collection in a hurry, money was nothing (and the kicks were free). Tales of dealers coughing up thousands for entire collections were not fiction. Donnie Perkins of Decatur, Georgia, spent four years acquiring 800 celebrity picks that he sold in one transaction for $3,000.

"Broke my heart because I had put so much time into finding them," said Perkins, whose collection was miniscule in comparison to that of supreme pick collector Paul Hettinger, who in 1990 began running monthly pick ads in *Goldmine*, an international magazine devoted to music business collectibles.

"There's no guide to picks," said Hettinger, a Winamac, Indiana, KISS fan who began saving picks in the '80s. "You get secondhand information and go from there. Collectors guard their sources."

Imprinted guitar picks started with Nick Lucas in the early 1930s. D'Andrea Manufacturing pioneered the general promotional pick business in 1938, offering up to 12 block letters a pick at 60 cents extra per gross. Musicians, guitar manufacturing companies and musical supply outlets soon took advantage of the offer. For decades the standard promo pick consisted of block letters die-printed on a celluloid plectrum. While jazz and orchestra guitarists utilized personalized picks, rock 'n' roll pickers were slower to catch on. Many legendary rock guitarists never had their own imprint. Jimi Hendrix used picks imprinted with "Manny's," a noted New York

An original Rick Nielsen Cheap Trick pick, which, more than some imprints, has lived up to its name.

City music emporium. But by the late 1970s rock musicians had joined the promo pick parade. Ten years later, personalized picks were standard operating procedure even among upstart acts.

The task of procuring an act's picks normally fell to the road manager or guitar technician. Promotional picks were available in ten gross minimums from a number of musical supply wholesalers around the country. In the case of Jim Dunlop USA and D'Andrea Manufacturing, large minimums could be ordered directly from the manufacturer. Jadee, Inc., a pick manufacturer out of Hebron, Illinois (bought by Gibson in 1994), found a niche in selling smaller minimum orders to licensed music dealers—as few as 100 picks imprinted with block letters. Meanwhile, a smattering of outfits such as Legend Picks, a custom design outfit out of Rock Island, Illinois, had found

their own niche selling signature and graphic logo picks to anyone in orders as small as one gross (see Appendix B).

Thus, if a roadie ordered a minimum of a particular imprint and never reordered more, that imprint became a de facto limited edition. In theory such a pick might increase in value. Van Halen was noted for changing imprints often, and hundreds of different Van Halen picks were floating around by the early '90s, some considered rare and valuable. At the other end of the scale were Rick Nielsen's original Cheap Trick picks, which were ordered and reordered in mass quantity and hurled to fans by the fistful. It's a fitting tribute that they gained a reputation as the cheapest of all possible collectible picks.

The '90s not only saw an explosion of rock, heavy-metal and country imprints, but a revolution in the way the imprint process was done. Using a variety of high-quality techniques, pick imprint makers could now produce an endless array of colorful, arty designs in a fraction of the time it once took to do common block letters.

This was both good and bad news for collectors. On one hand it meant a plethora of sensational picks to chose from, with new ones coming out daily. Otherwise, it meant celebrity imprints were easier to forge. Ordering mass

Left, Waylon Jennings; right, Johnny Cash.

quantities of plain, unmarked picks has always been a simple matter, and methods for adding an imprint abound. The infamous "S.R.V." affair was a perfect example. In early 1994 picks bearing Stevie Ray Vaughan's initials were supposedly circulating for $100 apiece. But they were deemed fakes, since the late, great guitar virtuoso apparently never ordered picks bearing his initials.

Left to right: Billy Ray Cyrus, Eric Clapton (not celluloid) and Guns & Roses.

Just how much of this sort of fakery was actually going on is a matter of conjecture. Certainly there was potential for chicanery. The technical ability to produce quality fake imprints—even exact duplicates of genuine promo imprints—was available to any inspired sociopath bent on mercenary musical mischief. And who really knows how many "genuine" imprints of a particular pick were made in the first place? Roadies come and go, records of their transactions are rarely, if ever, kept, and reordering is as easy as filling out a form. What's to prevent an enterprising guitar "techie" from ordering a thousand dollars' worth of extra picks for himself and selling them to the highest bidder? It isn't illegal. And who really cares?—especially if it's his own money and not the group's. The whole idea of promotional picks is to promote, after all.

In Atlanta, Georgia—a promo pick mecca—Jerry Coody opened Rock 'N' Roll Relics, possibly the first store in the country to specialize in celebrity picks. He explained the incentive for unscrupulous pick hawkers:

"I had two genuine Stevie Ray Vaughan picks that I couldn't sell at all before he died," said Coody, a former guitar technician with the Atlanta Rhythm Section. "Now, I could sell every one I got my hands on for $250 each."

Coody said most fake picks looked bogus because of sloppy workmanship. He also said that the motivation for making fake picks was reduced by the fact that flooding the market with a certain imprint would quickly drive the value of that pick down. Collectors knew what was rare and what wasn't. They also learned who to deal with and who to avoid. Still, Tony Weathers, a concert security worker in Atlanta and possibly the biggest promotional pick dealer in America, warned that fake picks were becoming widespread.

Left to right: KISS, Ricky Shelton and Chicago.

"Every day there's some kid getting screwed by somebody," said Weathers, who maintained a personal network of hundreds of collectors. "I only deal with roadies and techies, so I know for sure everything I sell is legitimate."

For some, at least, pick fever could be overwhelming. Erstwhile pick collector Donnie Perkins offered a stoic appraisal of the scene. "People grow up, get jobs, get married and have kids," he concluded. "Pick collectors get out of it after it's no fun anymore."

Chapter 10

A BRIEF HISTORY OF THUMB AND FINGER PICKS

While every plectrum is a pick, not every pick is a plectrum. Thumb and finger picks are not plectrums in the strictest sense. Fundamentally, plectrums are flat picks. Still, thumb and finger picks are so closely linked with blues, folk, country, bluegrass and Hawaiian music, they merit mention. Like plectrums, thumb and finger picks provide the tone of a stringed instrument. For that reason their importance should not be minimized. Furthermore, celluloid thumb picks predate celluloid mandolin, banjo or guitar plectrums, making them perhaps the first musical instrument accessory to use the first plastic.

Thumb-pick-style strumming and plucking devices have been around longer than their finger-picking counterparts and are associated with a number of instruments—steel and six-string guitars, zithers, autoharps and mountain dulcimers. It's possible that thumb picks of some sort were used to play the ancient psaltery, a zither-like instrument that flourished in Europe from the 12th century until the latter Middle Ages. Such picks could have been fashioned of wood, feather quills, ox horn, metal or other materials.

The 1897 Sears, Roebuck & Co. catalog listed thumb picks in both horn and celluloid, as well as brass autoharp "spirals" (worn on the index finger), nickel-plated "zither rings"

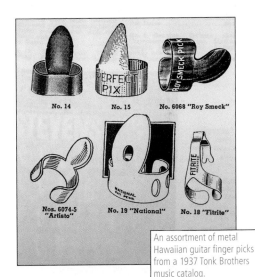

No. 14   No. 15   No. 6068 "Roy Smeck"

Nos. 6074-5 "Artisto"   No. 19 "National"   No. 18 "Fitrite"

An assortment of metal Hawaiian guitar finger picks from a 1937 Tonk Brothers music catalog.

A set of Golden Age Nick Manoloff metal thumb and finger picks.

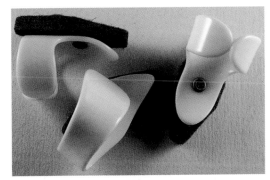

A set of uncommon celluloid/felt thumb and finger picks. Vintage unknown; probably from the Golden Age.

"The Wizard of the Strings": The late Roy Smeck in 1927.

The Herco Flat/Thumb guitar pick designed and introduced in 1984 by Jerry Hershman.

A 1933 dealer's catalog ad for the Roy Smeck Professional Hawaiian Guitar Outfit.

Above, a pair of Dobro transparent celluloid finger picks from the Golden Age.

The "world's first and only nylon thumb pick" made by Herco in "Bugablue" was unique because the nylon die to make it was so expensive.

(sharp-pointed thumb picks) and German silver "banjo thimbles" (forerunners of the modern finger pick).

The 1912 Gibson catalog offered celluloid "guitar thumb picks" that, it hastened to note, could be made to fit any thumb by heating the pick in hot water and bending it before "getting cool" (advice many Mississippi thumb-pickin' blues pioneers apparently took to heart—metaphorically, if not literally).

The traditional finger pick, a one-piece ring with a rounded tongue that fits under the fingertip below the first joint, achieved early fame as an accessory of the Hawaiian steel guitar. Such picks were advertised nationally by the Wurlitzer company in the early 1920s. However, similar finger "picks," "shields" and

"thimbles" had been around since before the turn of the century. Eventually, both finger and thumb picks were routinely used to play the banjo, Dobro, Spanish steel string guitar and Hawaiian guitar.

The person most responsible for popularizing thumb and finger picks was Roy Smeck, a 1920s vaudevillian, virtuoso and recording artist who could play practically anything that had a string attached to it—most notably the banjo, ukulele, guitar and Hawaiian guitar. Known as "The Wizard of the Strings," Smeck's name endorsed everything from guitars to banjos to the "Roy Smeck Professional Hawaiian Guitar Outfit" (two metal finger picks, a celluloid thumb pick and a metal slide bar, all for $1). Until the mid-1930s finger picks were

Left, a modern Dunlop south-paw thumb pick; right, a regular modern National thumb pick.

Above, four mosaic thumb picks, probably post-Golden Age. Below, four different "shell" thumb picks from the Golden Age.

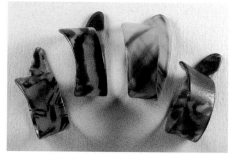

The first U.S. Postage Stamp to include a stringed instrument plectrum: Hank Williams, issued June 9, 1993, in Nashville, Tennessee. Stamp designed by Richard Waldrep of Baltimore, Maryland.

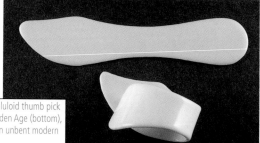

A vintage celluloid thumb pick from the Golden Age (bottom), along with an unbent modern counterpart.

almost always made of metal. Then, Dobro introduced its line of transparent celluloid finger picks, which was followed by other lines of celluloid finger picks, including those of the Oahu Publishing Co. of Cleveland, Ohio. Metal and cellulose-based plastics (usually celluloid) remained the primary thumb and finger pick materials throughout the 20th century (although in the mid-1970s Herco introduced "the world's first and only nylon thumb pick," colored in bright "Bugablue," a pick that could only be made from a special and extremely costly die).

Thumb and finger picks were sold by numerous American companies in the 1940s, '50s, and, thanks to the great folk music phenomenon, especially the '60s. They continued to be marketed by D'Andrea, National, Gibson, Kyser, Dunlop, Herco and other outfits throughout the '70s, '80s and '90s. Dunlop, which eventually bought Herco, offered the widest selection in both metal and plastic, and even sold a reverse thumb pick for south-paw pickers.

Other than minor modifications from time to time, the basic design of thumb and finger picks changed little over the years. Among the few notable exceptions were Luke Hart's triple-prong thumb pick, Porky Freeman's "Porky Pick" (a flat pick with a hook that attached to the thumb with a rubber band), and the aLasKa Pik, a "fingernail pick" designed to fit over the nail instead of the fingertip pad. Possibly the most practical modification was the Herco Flat/Thumb Guitar Pick—a standard celluloid flat pick with a thumb loop that was developed by Jerry Hershman in 1984. This combination thumb pick and flat pick—similar to an experimental model D'Andrea made for Chet Atkins in the late 1960s—came close to actually being both a thumb pick AND a plectrum.

Finger and thumb picks have played a meaningful role in the story of the 20th century guitar. Thumb picks were the first pick of any sort to pluck a guitar string. Such early blues, folk and country finger-picking influences as Blind Lemon Jefferson, Robert Johnson, Mississippi John Hurt and Riley Puckett used either thumb or finger picks, or both. In so doing, they paved the way for a plethora of guitar specialists—Rev. Gary Davis, Dave Van Ronk, Merle Travis, Taj Mahal, Ry Cooder and Chet Atkins, to name only a fraction of the instrumentalists who carried on the tradition.

Like plectrums, thumb and finger picks are seldom given much notice. But without them, the sound of popular music would indeed be noticeably diminished.

Picks as jewelry

Appendix A
PICKIN' PICKS

How essential is the role of the pick? According to at least two musicians who studied the question, the right pick can make all the difference.

In his book, *The Guitar*, renowned jazz guitarist Barney Kessel listed the importance of selecting the right pick as second only to that of selecting the right instrument.

"When we consider that each pick results in a different response from the player and a different sound to the listener, we can see how important pick selection is," he wrote.

Musician, writer and pick inventor John Pearse was even more explicit in his analysis, "A Word About Picks":

"A properly conceived pick can markedly improve the tonal response of an otherwise mediocre instrument—however, a bad pick could make your '39 Herringbone sound like something salvaged from a yard sale."

Both guitarists agreed that the crucial aspects to consider when selecting a pick are its shape, size and the material from which it is made.

"Picks come in so many shapes, sizes and thicknesses that it is difficult to classify them except for general recommendations," said Kessel. "The rest must be left to your experimentation.

"Generally speaking, large, heavy picks are for rhythm playing. They produce a loud, percussive sound, give long service even with vigorous use, and are easy to hold. They may be purchased in many shapes, (my favorite is a three-point triangle pick, in which I literally have three picks). While I use this pick mostly for rhythm, it gives a fat sound to single notes in playing passages not overly technical. It is made of celluloid, and I prefer it to the same pick in tortoise shell.

"To accompany a vocalist using an acoustic guitar, I recommend a pick of medium size and hardness. The pick should never feel awkward or heavy in the player's hand.

"…For electric guitar, particularly where solo work is involved, a small or medium size pick is preferable. Many guitarists prefer a soft or medium pick, but I prefer a hard pick.

"The pick should never be so thin that it creates a small, nasal sound, or so thick that it slaps the strings or creates a click from hitting the strings. You must choose according to your taste and needs the best pick for any particular musical situation…. A thin pick gets a small sound and wears out fast. A large pick is awkward to control in rapid passages…. Experiment until you find what you want."

What's the best pick material?

"Well," wrote John Pearse, "a marvelous material for pick use is tortoise shell; a chitinous substance that has an incredibly fast recovery time, can be easily shaped and is long wearing. However, it has been banned internationally and rightly so…. (Consequently), pick manufacturers have long been searching for some other substance with the same properties as tortoise shell.

"A material that was very much in vogue in the 1930s was celluloid. This made a wonderful pick, but, because of its chemical volatility—it had a nasty habit of bursting into flame if it got too hot—it fell out of favor. However, no other material that has been tried seems to be able to produce the richness of tone which you get from a shell or celluloid pick."

Still, there are musicians who swear by nylon, Delrin or any of the numerous other pick materials on the market.

Individual tastes vary. In the end, the best advice may be that offered by Barney Kessel back in 1967:

"Purchase a dozen picks made of different materials, and which vary in size, shape and thickness. Try them all, then write down your thoughts and evaluations about each after using it for at least two days.

"...Do not underestimate the importance of the pick in performance. It determines in large degree the kind of sound you'll get from your guitar, and the ease of your performance."

Note: Barney Kessel's book, *The Guitar*, is available through Criterion Music Corporation, 6124 Selma Avenue, Hollywood, CA 90028. 213-469-2296.

Information on John Pearse picks and guitar course available though John Pearse Strings, P.O. Box 295, Center Valley, PA 18034. 1-800-235-3302.

A FEW
USEFUL ADDRESSES

D'Andrea Manufacturing Co., Inc.
900 Shames Drive
Westbury, NY 11590
Ph: 516-997-8200

Dunlop Manufacturing, Inc.
P.O. Box 846
Benicia, CA 94510
Ph: 707-745-2722

Legend Picks
Custom Printed Guitar Picks
P.O. Box 3311
Rock Island, IL 61204
Ph: 319-344-9036

Light Impressions
Resource and Archival Supplies
439 Monroe Avenue
Rochester, NY 14603
Ph: 1-800-828-6216

Novus, Inc.
Makers of Novus Plastic Polish No. 2
Minneapolis, MN 55438
Ph: 1-800-548-6872

1928 D'Andrea Catalog Selections

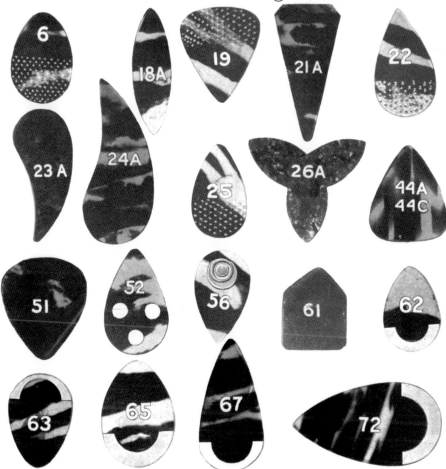

Picks are shown at 90% of catalog size.

1946-47 D'Andrea Catalog Selections

No. 317G

No. 318G

No. 319G

No. 320G

No. 317½G

No. 318½G

No. 320½G

The Cushion Grip is a rubber band stretched across top of pick.
Making pick non skid. For the professional.

These cushion grip celluloid picks
are finished and beveled.

No. 84

Picks are shown at 75% of catalog size.

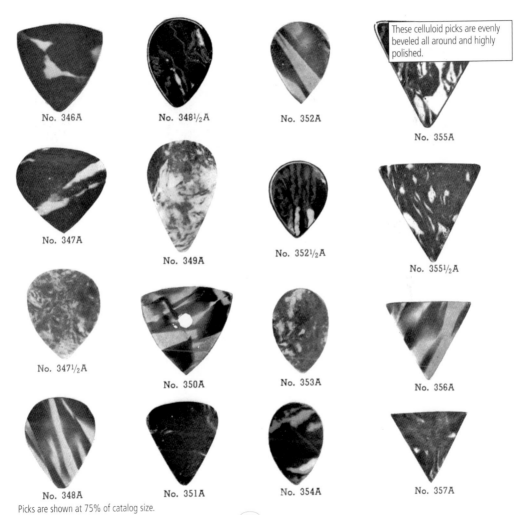

No. 346A

No. 348½A

No. 352A

These celluloid picks are evenly beveled all around and highly polished.

No. 355A

No. 347A

No. 349A

No. 352½A

No. 355½A

No. 347½A

No. 350A

No. 353A

No. 356A

No. 348A

No. 351A

No. 354A

No. 357A

Picks are shown at 75% of catalog size.

99

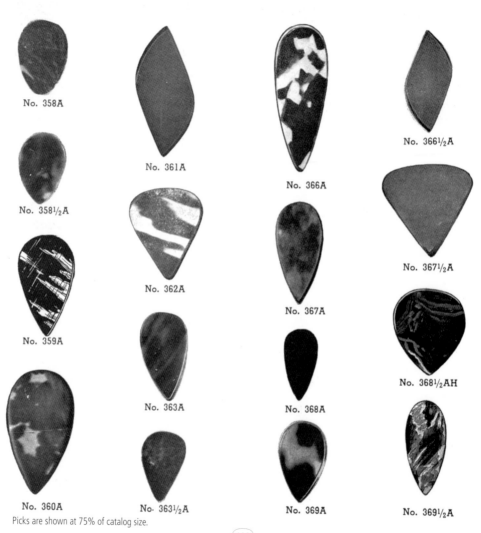

No. 358A

No. 358½A

No. 359A

No. 360A

No. 361A

No. 362A

No. 363A

No. 363½A

No. 366A

No. 367A

No. 368A

No. 369A

No. 366½A

No. 367½A

No. 368½AH

No. 369½A

Picks are shown at 75% of catalog size.

Yet another idea to make certain a pick sticks to business. These Grip-It picks from Steve Clayton Inc. have their own, built-in adhesive.

BIBLIOGRAPHY

Books:

Acoustic Guitars and Other Fretted Instruments. George Gruhn and Walter Carter. San Francisco, California: Miller Freeman, Inc. 1993.

ASCAP Biographical Dictionary, 4th ed. New York: R.R. Bowker. 1980.

The Billboard Book of Number One Hits, 3rd ed. Fred Bronson. New York: Billboard. 1992.

The Book of Firsts. Patrick Robertson. New York: Clarkson N. Potter, Inc. 1974.

Discovering Great Singers of Classical Pop. Roy Hemming and David Hajdu. New York: Newmarket Press. 1991.

The Early Mandolin. James Taylor and Paul Sparks. New York: Oxford Press. 1989.

Encyclopedia of The 20th Century. John Drexel, ed. New York: Facts On File. 1991.

Extraordinary Origins of Everyday Things. Charles Panati. New York: Harper & Row. 1987.

Gibsons Fabulous Flat-top Guitars: An Illustrated History & Guide. Eldon Whitford, David Vinopal and Dan Erlewine. San Francisco: Miller Freeman Books. 1994.

The Great Song Thesaurus, 2nd ed. Roger Lax and Frederick Smith. New York: Oxford Press. 1989.

The Guitar. Barney Kessel. Hollywood, California: Windsor Music Co. 1967.

The Guitar Players. James Sallis. Lincoln, Nebraska: University of Nebraska Press. 1994.

Hot Licks. Jim Hatlo, ed. Cupertino, California: GPI Publications. 1989.

I Hear America Talking: An Illustrated History of American Words and Phrases. Stuart Berg Flexner. New York: Simon and Schuster. 1976.

Industrial Plastics: Theory and Application, 2nd ed. Terry L. Richardson. Albany, New York: Delmar Publishers, Inc. 1989.

I Remember Distinctly—A Family Album of The American People in The Years of Peace: 1918 to Pearl Harbor. Agnes Rogers and Frederick Lewis Allen. New York: Harper & Brothers Publishers. 1947.

Kaman Music Reference Manual & Music Products Catalog. Bloomfield, Connecticut: Kaman Music. 1993.

Listening to America: An Illustrated History of Words and Phrases from Our Lively and Splendid Past. Stuart Berg Flexner. New York: Simon and Schuster. 1982.

Pioneer Plastic: The Making and Selling of Celluloid. Robert Friedel. Madison, Wisconsin: University of Wisconsin Press. 1983.

Plastics As An Art Form. Thelma R. Newman. Philadelphia: Chilton Books. 1964.

The Role of Rock: A Guide to The Social and Political Consequences of Rock Music. Don J. Hibbard and Carol Kaleialoha. Englewood Cliffs, New Jersey: Prentice-Hall, Inc. 1983.

Top 40 Hits, 5th ed. Joel Whitburn. New York: Billboard 1992.

Whatever Became of…. 4th series. Richard Lamparski. New York: Crown Publishers, Inc. 1973.

The World Almanac Book of Inventions. Valérie-Anne Giscard d'Estaing. New York: World Almanac Publications. 1985.

Articles:

"All Those Fabulous Picks!" Jas Obrecht. *Guitar Player*: May, 1990.

"Bakelite Plastics." R.J. Klimpert. *20th Century Guitar*: January/February, 1992.

"Collecting Vintage Guitars." Craig Wyatt. *Today's Collector*: August, 1994.

"Gibson: 1900 through 1942." George Gruhn. *Vintage Guitar*: January, 1994.

"The History of The Vintage Market." George Gruhn. *Vintage Guitar*: May, 1994.

"Nick Lucas: The Artist Behind The Name." Mark Humphrey. *Frets*: April, 1980.

"One Word: Plastics." R.J. Klimpert. *20th Century Guitar*: November/December, 1991.

"The Picks of Rock And Roll." Steve Rosen. *Guitar Player*: July, 1975.

"Plastics: Acrylic." R.J. Klimpert. *20th Century Guitar*: July/August, 1992.

Index

Will Hoover is an award-winning journalist living in Hawaii. He is a former Epic recording artist, ASCAP Award-winning songwriter and Nashville studio musician. In this photo, he holds the first Kamaka Pineapple Ukulele ever made.
Photo by Take Umeda